Breaking the Eve Mentality

Breaking the Eve Mentality

DEBORAH G. HUNTER

Hunter Heart Publishing
DuPont, Washington 98327

Breaking the Eve Mentality
2nd Edition

Copyright© 2009 Deborah G. Hunter
Original copyright © 2006
ISBN: 978-0-6151-8180-6

Hunter Heart Publishing, LLC
P.O. Box 354
DuPont, Washington 98327
www.hunterheartpublishing.com

Cover designer: Exousia Marketing Group, LLC
www.exousiamg.com

All Scripture quotations, unless otherwise indicated are taken from the New King James Version of the Bible, Copyright © 1982 by Thomas Nelson, Inc. Used by permission. All rights reserved.

Quotations from King James Bible have been denoted *(KJV)* taken from the Holy Bible, King James Version.

"Scripture taken from The Message. Copyright © 1993, 1994, 1995, 1996, 2000, 2001, 2002. Used by permission of NavPress Publishing Group."

Scripture quotations marked *NLT* are taken from the Holy Bible, New Living Translation, Copyright © 1996. Used by permission of Tyndale House Publishers, Inc., Wheaton, Illinois, 60189. All rights reserved.

Foreword: Scripture taken from the HOLY BIBLE, NEW INTERNATIONAL VERSION®. Copyright © 1973, 1978, 1984 International Bible Society. Used by permission of Zondervan. All rights reserved.

Hebrew and Greek words taken from Strong's Exhaustive Concordance of the Bible together with Dictionaries of the Hebrew and Greek Words by James Strong, S.T.D., LL.D. Hendrickson Publishers.

The word satan is not capitalized in this work. This does defy the basic rules of grammatical expression, but we have chosen not to highlight this name due to the nature of his character. There are instances of capitalization throughout the text that are used to emphasize the nature of certain statements.

ISBN 13: 978-0-9823944-7-2

Printed in the United States of America

This book or parts thereof may not be reproduced in any form, stored in a retrieval system, or transmitted in any form by any means- electronic, mechanical, photocopy, recording or otherwise- without prior permission of the publisher, except as provided by United States of America copyright law.

Dedication

I acknowledge first, my Lord and Savior, Jesus Christ, for saving me and turning my life back to the One in whom it was intended for. I dedicate this to You.

My deepest gratitude to one of my spiritual mothers, Pastor Linda Magee, who opened my eyes to my unsubmissiveness and not only taught me, but showed me how to be a submissive woman in my marriage, as well as in the house of the Lord. I can never repay you for what you have imparted into my life. I can only take what you have taught me, and be all that God created for me to be, and to do all that He purposed for me to do. I love you.

To Rosalind Johnson, I send a shout out to God to bless you for your selfless acts of love and intercession for me. Your words of encouragement during the trials in my marriage lifted me up and gave me the courage to press on. You are a *"PRAYER WARRIOR"*.

To Sabrina Paige, whose wisdom and testimony made a lasting impression in my spirit. You were like a mother to me when I needed it the most. May God richly bless you.

To Shasta Gary, my best friend and sister in Christ, who displayed submissiveness and faithfulness in a way that I have never seen before? God will bless you and honor you. He is the God of Reconciliation.

To my mother-in-law, Diane Hunter, who shared her wisdom with me, and taught me how to be a wife to her son through her own example of being a submissive woman. I am ever so grateful to have you as a "second" mom.

To my mother Dean Greer; for living out your vows to my father up until the very end of his life. You planted seeds in my life that will never die. I love you Mom.

Finally, yet importantly, I dedicate this book to my husband Chris. You stood by me at times when I really did not deserve it. You put up with a lot, and I can only thank you for sticking around, so that God could birth this book, and change me in the process. You are an awesome man of God, and I am proud to have you as my head. I am so looking forward to what God has in store for our family. I love you sweetheart.

Acknowledgments

To Pastors Will and Kristie Moreland and the Victory Through Faith Christian Fellowship family for holding me accountable to the birthing of this book. God will honor your faithfulness. We truly *"Live In Victory Everyday"*.

To Pastors Daryl and Linda Magee and the New Covenant Christian Fellowship family for showing me that we need one another in order to carry out God's plan in the Earth. You have changed my life.

To Bishop Steven W. and Dr. Keira Taylor-Banks and the Living Waters Christian Fellowship family for all of their prayers and support for my family and I. You were our firm foundation, and the Lord has continued to build upon it. We are walking in the prosperity that you prophesied over our lives. We love you all with the love of the Lord.

Last, but definitely not the least, my two angels from heaven, Jade and Elijah. I know this book took a lot of my time away from you two, but God says obedience is better than sacrifice. I know that the blessing of the Lord flows from the head, down the beard, and onto the skirts of the garment. You are blessed and you WILL walk in the predestined purposes for your lives. Mommy loves you both dearly.

Foreword

Debbie has her finger on the pulse of many believers in the church today. Breaking the "Eve" Mentality is a back to basics manual. It is an insightful look into the hearts and minds of many in the body of Christ. The art of submission is something that should be nourished, developed, and practiced by everyone in the church, and in society as a whole. Our Lord submitted His will unto the Father's even unto the point of His death on the cross. Thank God for Jesus who came to redeem us! We should follow His lead.

> *Your attitude should be the same as that of Jesus Christ: Who being in very nature God, did not consider equality with God something to be grasped, but made Himself nothing, taking the very nature of a servant, being made in human likeness. And being found in appearance as a man, He humbled Himself and became obedient to death_even death on a cross! (Philippians 2:5-8, NIV)*

Pastor Linda G. Magee

Co-Pastor/ New Covenant Christian Fellowship
Vilseck, Germany

Introduction

As I began to write this book, the Holy Spirit dropped so many things into my spirit concerning submission. I thought I knew what it meant to be submissive. I saw myself as a true woman of God, and never would have thought that I lacked in this area. After being led to Germany, and sitting under the teachings of an awesome man and woman of God, I slowly started to see that what I believed of myself was inaccurate. The Word of God began to peel away layers of pride that I did not know existed in my life. As time went on, I found myself being broken on many occasions. My first lady prayed over me, and revealed to me that I was not being submissive. I received it, and went home completely changed, or at least I thought I was.

Time after time, I found myself back where I started. I could not understand why things were not changing in my marriage or in my walk with the Lord. I prayed, read daily, interceded for people, and truly loved my brothers and sisters, but something was wrong, and I could not figure out what that something was. I truly desired a relationship with my husband that was different from any other. I wanted us to share a closeness that would strengthen not only us, but our children's lives as well. One that would give our children the foundation they needed to help them grow into the man and woman that God purposed for them to be. I wanted our marriage to be an example to others who thought that there was no help for theirs. I concluded that I was doing everything right in my marriage.

All of my motives felt right to me. I wanted the best for my husband, my children, and everyone that was dear to me. Therefore, I started to blame my husband for our marriage not growing. I wanted him to stand up and be the man God wanted him to be over our family. What I did not realize, at the time, was that I had a spirit attached to me. For the purpose of this book, I call it the *"Eve Mentality"*.

If you noticed, the word I was used many times in the beginning of this text. The Holy Spirit revealed to me that I was not seeking what the Lord wanted for my marriage, my children, and my ministry, but what I wanted them to be. I had already purposed in my mind that I was a godly woman, and that I had nothing but good intentions for everything that I did. I saw myself as a good person, but what I did not see was that *sneaky, cunning*, and *manipulative* spirit called *PRIDE*. It seeped into my life unbeknownst to me, and became like a cancer.

Many times cancer can grow for years inside of a person before they realize that they have it. This is what happened to me. I could not figure out how this started in me, because I could recognize the spirit of pride a mile away *(now I see why)*. I had to humble myself, and allow God to break me to find out where this spirit originated. It took a lot of breaking in many different areas of my life, because where the pride started, is not where it ended up. Remember, pride is like a cancer, it spreads to every area of your life. I thank God for placing a woman of God in my life who was bold. She did not sugarcoat anything that she said to me. She poured wisdom into my situations, and it began to drown out that wicked spirit of pride that I allowed into my life.

Throughout this book, you will begin to see how easy it is for pride to creep into your life. One scripture that the Holy Spirit revealed to me during this process that has truly blessed and changed my life is 2 Corinthians 13:5, which says:

> "Examine yourselves to see if your faith is genuine. Test yourselves. If you cannot tell that Jesus Christ is among you, it means you have failed the test."(NLT)

This translation shot through my spirit more than any other, because of the use of the word *genuine*. We have to know that whatever we say we are doing in the name of Jesus that it is really about Him and not about us. I pray that this book opens the eyes of your understanding as it did mine. Humble yourselves and allow the Holy Spirit to minister to your life situations.

> *Without humbleness, there can be no brokenness, and without brokenness, there can be no deliverance.* _D.G. Hunter

Prepare yourself to break out of the *"Eve Mentality"* and receive your *Victory* through submission.

Table of Contents

Chapter 1: In the Beginning…as it is Now, *1*

Chapter 2: Understanding Submission, *15*

Chapter 3: The Spirit of Pride, *23*

Chapter 4: Submission in Marriage: The Role of the Woman, *41*

Chapter 5: Submission in Marriage: The Role of the Man, *65*

Chapter 6: Submission: Holding One Another Accountable, *83*

Chapter 7: Submission to Authority, *89*

Chapter 8: Submission in the Church, *99*

Chapter 9: Submitting to the Will of God, *117*

Chapter 10: Victory through Submission, *131*

Notes, *139*

"True strength lies in *submission* which permits one to dedicate his life, through devotion, to something beyond himself."

~Henry Miller

Chapter 1
In the Beginning...as it is Now

Paradise

As I meditate on how it was in the beginning, at creation, the only word that comes to my mind is *peace*. I picture in my mind the tranquility in the Garden of Eden, how the trees stand tall above the ground with leaves cascading down to the earth beneath. I see flowers of every type that possess colors that I have never seen before, whose smell my senses cannot comprehend. The streams of running water that I hear have not an end, but are eternal in their orchestration. The animals, every species ever created, are all on one accord; peaceable and having purpose. I see Adam walking through the Garden, as all of creation bows in reverence to his authority. I imagine such a peace in the midst of the Garden; tranquility far beyond anything I can ever know or experience. I see order and purpose to everything God created, and it is lovely.

My minds eye could not fathom how satan so easily tempted Eve when she was living in total bliss. She was the mother of all living. She and Adam had dominion over every living thing ever created, but this was not enough for her. Satan came quickly and seized the moment when Eve was without Adam. When I say without Adam, I mean that she chose to have her own mind, instead of bringing it under submission to her head and to her Creator. He used her will and her knowledge of the tree of good and evil against her.

Notice in Genesis 3:1 that the serpent asks Eve, *"Has God indeed said, 'You shall not eat of every tree of the garden?"* Satan was not sure of what God had told Adam and Eve, so he, in his cunningness, persuaded her to tell him of which tree they were forbidden to eat from. This is how the enemy operates. He does not know the plans God has for you, unless you give place to him. If satan had known that the crucifying of Christ would bring salvation to the world, he would have tried to move mountains to stop it from happening.

The Failed Test

Eve failed her test in many ways. First, Eve lost sight of her position in the Garden. The Word of God shows that they were given a position *above* the creatures of the earth, and that they were to have dominion over them.

> *"Then God blessed them, and said to them, be fruitful and multiply; fill the earth and subdue it; have dominion over the birds of the air, and over every living thing that moves on the earth." (Genesis 1:28)*

Adam and Eve had authority over the creatures of the earth. Eve, blinded by the serpent's guile, forgot that she had the power to subdue it. Furthermore, Eve accepted what the serpent said to be true without consulting with Adam, her head. She assumed a position that she was not equipped to handle. God created her as a companion and a co-ruler for Adam, not as one making life altering decisions, especially without guidance from her head. We are not aware of how Eve felt by making this decision, but what we do know from reading the Word of God is that God did not create confusion, but satan.

> *"For God is not the author of confusion but of peace, as in all the churches of the saints." (1 Corinthians 14:33)*

Eve stepped into rebellion, because of what we call the *"I"* syndrome. The serpent said to Eve,

> *"YOU will not surely die, for in the day YOU eat of it YOUR eyes will be opened and YOU will be like God, knowing good and evil."(Genesis 3:4-5- Emphasis added is mine.)*

Satan had already mapped out a plan to destroy the unity of marriage between man and woman, as well as the covenant between God and man by emphasizing to Eve that it was *"ALL ABOUT HER"*. We should not be so naïve in recognizing the character of satan when we see it. This was why he fell from grace with God, because it was all about him, instead of being all about God. Ultimately, Eve failed by not trusting and believing her Creator. This is probably the single most important test that she failed. God specifically said to Adam in Genesis 2: 16-17,

> *"And the Lord God commanded the man, saying 'Of every tree of the garden thou mayest freely eat: But of the tree of the knowledge of good and evil, thou shalt not eat of it: for in the day that thou eatest thereof, thou shalt surely die."(KJV)*

This was a command of God, not a suggestion. Even though Eve had not yet been created, she was evidently informed along the way that this was not acceptable. Instead of believing the Word of God, which had authority, she moved out on the word of the serpent that had to ask her what God had said. *My God!* This should have been the deciding factor in Eve's decision to subdue the serpent, but it became all about Eve, instead of all about God.

Breaking the Ranks

Eve failed to maintain her position, under the covering of her husband, Adam, and of the Word of God, and assumed for herself a new role. My friend, it is absolutely imperative that we know what our position is in the natural, as well as the spiritual. Satan can only come in and confuse a situation when we are not in our designated positions. When I looked up the word position in the dictionary, the definition was *the right or appropriate place*. Another definition was *a strategic area occupied by someone*. If we would come to realize that there is a right and appropriate place for us, then we would not make half as many mistakes as we do in the natural, as well as the spiritual. All that Eve needed to do was to know that she was Adam's companion, someone in whom he could share God's blessings, and that she was equally, with Adam, given dominion over every living creature.

As I meditated on the word position, defined *as a strategic area occupied by someone*, the Holy Spirit revealed to me that God intended for Adam and Eve to live in this way. He gave them dominion over all creatures in the air, in the waters, and on the earth. He gave them authority over all things, and Eve handed that authority right over to satan when she broke the ranks. No matter how good something looks to us or how appealing an opportunity may be, we have to analyze ourselves and make sure that it will not move us out of our positions. If it does, then it is not from God. Take into consideration, not only yourself, but everyone who is directly or indirectly in the line of fire. We sometimes think that when we are faced with a decision, that it will only affect us, but this is far from the truth. Our spouses, our children, our co-workers, our fellow believers, and even our leaders can be indirectly in the path of our disobedience.

Eve did not consider who would suffer because of her decision to eat from the tree of the knowledge of good and evil. The Bible says that Adam was there with Eve when she ate of the fruit, but why did he not stop her from doing so? Was it that he knew of one's free will to choose? Did he love her so much that he refused to step over her decision? Or was Adam himself tempted, just as Eve was? Adam could have refused, but he did not, therefore causing the fall of man. Eve's decision not only affected her husband and herself, but ultimately, all of humankind. Eve wanted to possess the wisdom in which the serpent spoke of. She desired it, and allowed her desires to cloud her judgment; therefore, causing her to lose her position in the Garden.

Issues of the Heart

When God summoned Adam in the Garden and said, *"Where are you?"(Genesis 3:9)*, God was not asking him of his location, because He is the Omnipresent God; everywhere at all times. He was inquiring of Adam where he was at in relationship to Him. Notice that God did not call out to Eve, but Adam. God knew that the relationship had been broken. The relationship had been compromised, because of Adam's disobedience, not Eve's. Adam told God that he was afraid and hid himself. We cannot hide from the face of God or from the responsibilities that He places in our hands.

> *"The eyes of the Lord are in every place, keeping watch on the evil and the good."(Proverbs 15:3)*

Immediately, Adam placed the blame on Eve and in return, she accused the serpent of deceiving her. This is how the enemy causes derision among us. He knows that we do not like to admit that anything is our fault. We try to find someone whom we can shift the blame. What I saw in this verse was that Eve admitted that the serpent deceived her. Even though she blamed him, she acknowledged his deception of her. The serpent did not say a word, because it could not. It recognized the authority of God. *Hallelujah!* God gave this authority to Adam and Even freely. They were to bring all things under their subjection; instead, they turned it over to the enemy. It is amazing to see that the serpent recognized the Lord as sovereign. He was the only one who did not pass blame or give an excuse.

We have to look within ourselves and ask many tough questions. *Do the decisions in my life rest solely on me, or do I have someone who can help me? Can I make those decisions alone and it only affect me? Are my motives for making choices on my own selfish? Am I afraid that if I let someone else make a decision for me, I will have to submit to him or her?* I challenge you this day to ask yourself these questions. Once you have uncovered the answers, you will be able to recognize if you possess the *"Eve Mentality"*.

Recognizing the "Eve" Mentality

The fall of humankind originated with Eve, the mother of all living. God passed down judgment, because of disobedience by Eve, as well as Adam, but the Word specifies to whom the deceit was credited to.

> *"And Adam was not deceived, but the woman being deceived, fell into transgression." (1Timothy 2:14)*

Eve set in motion the paths that we are walking in today in our lives. Through her act of disobedience, she broke the covenant between not only her and husband, but led the revolt between man and God. She did not think of the consequences before she made such a life-altering decision, and she was judged accordingly.

> *"To the woman He said: I will greatly multiply your sorrow and your conception; In pain you shall bring forth children; your desire will be for your husband, and he shall rule over you." (Genesis 3:16)*

This scripture solidifies God's judgment over her disobedience, which shows us that His intentions for marriage were not as we see them operating today. She set the stage for the struggles that we, as women, go through in our marriages. God said that when we desire our husbands; when we want intimacy, kindness, compassion, friendship, and communication, our husband's would rule over us. Our desires would not be reciprocated the way that we would want them to be. I do not know about you, but this is a very frustrating way to live? We have to understand that in the beginning there was order and purpose to everything God created, and that divine order was broken. We should not complain or inquire of God why we have to suffer because of Eve's sin. Yes, sin entered the world through her disobedience, but we have received the living Word as our guide on how to live godly lives now and for peace to be restored to our marriages through the sacrifice of Jesus Christ.

We cannot change past circumstances, or the fact that sin dwells in our flesh, but what we can do is *"deny ourselves, take up His cross and follow Him"(Luke 9:23).* We have to understand that we are but flesh, and only through Jesus can we be cleansed of the evil that dwells in our hearts. It is easy to blame someone else for our problems, as Adam and Eve did, but by doing this, we exclude ourselves from being delivered by a merciful God. Eve is the easy target, but we are the *BULLSEYE!* God holds us individually accountable for our actions. He will not accept our excuses as to why we are not responsible for them.

Taking on the Spirit of Eve

From the beginning of the sacred act of marriage, we have seen people become ecstatic at the thought of marrying their *"soul mate"*. As children, we act out the roles of husband and wife by putting on our mother's dress and high heels and our father's hat and tie. We find some flowers, and look for rice to throw as we walk down our make believe aisle. As children, we had such an innocent perception of what marriage was supposed to be. We looked up to our parents, and marveled at them as they gave one another a kiss or held one another's hand. There is something so comforting about seeing this as a child. It is the foundation of what we expect our own marriages to be, but the sad reality is that the perfection we see as children does not exist.

We take these perceptions of marriage into our relationships, and feel as if we are the only couple on this earth, like Adam and Eve were. We live for every moment together; holding one another, taking walks together, and sitting on the couch watching movies all night, until we fall asleep in the arms of one another. No one can get in touch with either one of you, because you are spending every waking moment together. We cannot get enough of one another. We allow ourselves to be so caught up in the clouds that we lose sight of reality, and the reality is that you did not fall in love with this person; you fell into *lust* with them.

> *"So the woman saw that the tree was good for food, that it was pleasant to the eyes, and a tree desirable to make one wise, she took of its fruit and ate. She also gave to her husband, and he ate." (Genesis 3:6)*

What Eve saw with her eyes made her want it even though she knew that God had forbidden it? The majority of people who get married do so, because of an attraction to the other person, not because of love. It starts out with that first look. Then desire begins to rise within you, and now you want them. You will do anything, including marrying someone who you do not love to get it. What is this *"IT"?* It is called *lust.*

> *"For all that is in this world-the lust of the flesh, the lust of the eyes and the pride of life-is not of the Father, but is of the world." (1 John 2:16)*

Lust formed in Eve's heart when she saw that the tree was good. She allowed the serpent; gave him place, to show her that the tree was good. If Eve knew who she was, who God created her to be, she would not have allowed the serpent to deceive her. This is a very important point, because if we know who we are, we will not allow just anyone into our lives, let alone marry them. Satan knows that our flesh is weak, and that if he can get to us early on, he will seize that moment to tempt us.

What fascinated me when reading in Genesis about the creation of Eve, was that immediately after God formed her and said in verse 24, *"Therefore a man shall leave his father and mother and be joined to his wife, and they shall be one flesh"*, the serpent came. Now, we do not know the specific timeline of events in scripture between verse 24 of Genesis Chapter 2 and Chapter 3 verse 1, but we are to assume that it was not a long period.

This is how the enemy operates. He is cunning and full of guile. We can coin his character, or at least one of his attributes, as being *sneaky like a fox*. Satan knew that if Adam and Eve truly became one flesh, walked in one accord, and firmly trusted God's Word, he was in trouble. That is why he had to move quickly to reach Eve and distract her. We find that as soon as we receive a word from God, the enemy comes to steal that word. We have to be in position, and not distracted, so that we can hold that word in our heart and stand firm against the tricks of the enemy.

In Genesis 3:5-7, satan told Eve, *"For God knows that in the day you eat of it your eyes will be opened, and you will be like God, knowing good and evil."* God did not want Adam and Eve's eyes to be opened to see in this way. That is why He forbade them to eat of this tree. Satan twists the Word of God for his own pleasure. If we were to see a passage written by satan it would probably say, *"For Satan knows that in the day You eat of it, Your eyes will be opened, and You will be just like Satan, knowing sin and evil."*

The Opened Door

Eve opened a door that God intentionally left closed for her benefit. This mentality is described best as, *"I know what is best for me." "I do not need anyone to tell me how to run my life, how to walk, how to talk, or even who to marry"*. Eve forgot that it was God who reached inside of Adam to pull her out. She was not her own person, but an intricate piece of someone else. *Glory to God!* We need to catch hold of this revelation. We cannot think that the decisions we make only affect us, because we are connected in the Spirit to many other souls.

"For you died, and your life is hidden with Christ in God." (Colossians 3:3)

Our lives are no longer our own. When we gave our lives to God, we traded our life for something new, and we cannot turn back to our old way of thinking, because every choice we make has a consequence. Eve did not take into consideration that *ALL* of humankind would suffer, because of her disobedience.

If you are like most people in this world, you have struggled with finding out what your purpose in this life is. We grow up knowing that we are supposed to go to school and get good grades. We graduate high school and enter college looking to make a good career for ourselves, so that we can become financially stable. After we have settled in our careers, we venture out to find someone in whom we can share our lives with, and ultimately have children. Many of us miss more than a few of these objectives, and take different courses in our lives. We may have been re-routed, because we came up against some roadblocks along the way, so we refuse to go back and try to accomplish what we had originally set our goals to be. We begin to settle for an easy way out, or better, an easy way into something new.

God purposed a life for each one of us to walk in. God's Word in Proverbs 19:21 says, *"You can make many plans, but the Lord's purpose will prevail."(NLT)* We can make as many plans as we like, but no matter what we choose; God has already chosen our paths. As we lose our way in life, we become impatient, and refuse to seek God on what to do next. We fail to understand that He has intentionally turned us around, because of something that we missed before. His Will is not for us to move on to something new, until we have done what He has asked us to do first. Many of us miss this revelation, and move out in our flesh, because we do not have the time or patience to go back and start again.

> *"Be anxious for nothing, but in everything, through prayer and supplication, with thanksgiving, let your requests be made known to God."(Philippians 4:6)*

Just because we do not know what to do next does not mean that God does not. We have to trust Him, and wait on Him, so that our result is His will for us. Please hear me when I say this, God loves us so much that He will stop us dead in our tracks when we are going down the wrong road. Some of us do not see this as God intervening on our behalf, but as an opportunity for us to look elsewhere. Stay focused on His will for your life and you will not make many of the mistakes that you have in the past. He loves us so much that He will give us a second, third, and even fourth chance to get it right. Receive the correction of the Lord, and have faith that He knows what is best for you. Do not allow doors to open that are not *ready* to be opened.

> *"Nor give place to the devil."(Ephesians 4:27)*

As soon as you open a door that God has willed to be closed, you allow the enemy to come in. As I said before, Eve gave place to satan. She allowed an opportunity for the devil to enter in, because she moved ahead of God.

As I sought the Holy Spirit's thoughts on these *"open doors"*, He revealed to me that when it is God opening a door for us, all that we have to do is walk through it, because there will be nothing blocking our way. *Hallelujah!* This should be a clear sign that God is working in our lives, but we continue to push against the doors that He is intentionally leaving shut for our benefit. We can continue pushing, until God will *allow* the doors to be opened. He is a God that gives us free will to choose which way we want to go. He will not stop us if we continue to pursue our own way of doing things.

Once we have allowed the doors to be opened, we have let satan enter in to tempt us with situations that God did not intend for us to be in. God will take us down certain paths in our lives for a reason. He knows each of us by name, and has a purpose specifically for each of us. So, if He chooses to close a door in your life, receive it, and wait patiently on Him to reveal the next step.

> *"While we were children, our parents did what seemed best to them. But God is doing what is best for us, training us to live God's holy best."(Hebrews 12:10, NLT)*

Do not refuse the correction that God is placing in your life. He is allowing this to happen, because He knows what you need. Humble yourself under His mighty hand, and let Him do a perfect work in you.

We saw from Genesis Chapter 3 that Eve, even though she knew that she was not to eat of the tree of the knowledge of good and evil, took it upon herself to do so, and in doing so, let the enemy in. It is a very dangerous thing to believe in your instincts or better yet, other people who tell you to do things that you have not consulted with God in regards to.

This is why the enemy does not want us in relationship with the Father. Once we have established a personal relationship with Jesus Christ, His Spirit leads us, or at least it should. The Holy Spirit guides our decisions, and causes us to test situations to see if they are from God or not.

> *"Trust in the Lord with all your heart and lean not on your own understanding. In all your ways acknowledge Him and He will direct your paths." (Proverbs 3:5-6)*

We have to know who our God is and what He has already done for us, as His children. He is not only *Jehovah-Jireh*, the Lord our provider, but He is *Jehovah-nissi*, the Lord our banner. He protects us, and lifts us up over our situations, so that we do not fall in them. He knows when to open doors and when to shut them.

> *"And to the angel of the church in Philadelphia write, 'These things says He, who is holy, He who is true, He who has the key of David, He who opens and no one shuts, and shuts and no one opens." (Revelation 3:7)*

Allow God to direct you in every area of your life, and refuse to move, until you hear from Him. I guarantee you that your life will have much more peace if you wait patiently on the Father.

Chapter 2
Understanding Submission

The "Taboo" of Submission

If you speak the word submission in any area, whether it is marriage, the workplace, or even in the church, you had better get ready to debate, or even worse, get into a heated discussion with someone. No one wants to hear about submission, because of the *"taboo"* it has carried for years, decades, and even centuries. Submitting to another person is unheard of for many people. For years, this word has been twisted and used to suit individual needs, whatever they may be.

The word submission is defined as *the act of lowering oneself, being submissive, humble or compliant; submitting to the authority or control of another*. We may as well put this book down now and stop reading, because the definition itself causes our flesh to rise up. We cannot even fathom the thought of lowering ourselves to someone else or allowing them to control us.

We have to pull ourselves away from the way the *"world"* sees things and find out how God sees them. The word submission is derived from the Greek word *hupotasso*, which means *to be subordinate; to obey; to be under obedience, put under, subdue unto, (be, make) subject (to, unto), be (put) in subjection (to, under) or submit self unto*. To many, even this definition causes us to rise in opposition. We are a people who want things how we want them. We will do everything possible to obtain what we want in this life, no matter what it costs or whom it hurts to get it.

The origin of a word in the Bible goes back to what some call the *law of first reference*. This is where a word is used for the first time in scripture. From here is where a word's origin takes root; has its foundation. Anytime you see this word again in scripture, you should reference it back to the first time it was used.

> *"Then God blessed them, and God said to them, 'Be fruitful and multiply; fill the earth and subdue it, have dominion over the fish of the sea, over the birds of the air, and over every living thing that moves on the earth." (Genesis 1:28)*

The word subdue here is derived from the Hebrew word *kabash*, which means *to tread down; disregard; to conquer, subjugate, violate: bring into bondage, force, keep under, subdue, bring into subjection*. This is how God commanded Adam and Eve to live in the earth. He wanted them to bring *ALL* things under subjection to them. God knew that this was necessary, because He is a God of order and if this order is broken, the enemy can move his way in.

The word dominion in the same verse is derived from the Hebrew word *radah*, which also means *to tread down; to subjugate, to prevail against, reign, rule over, or take*. These two words have an aspect of authority that only God can give. If Adam and Eve would have taken on this privileged authority, satan would not have been able to tell the difference between their voice and the voice of God, and he would have immediately fled their presence. *Glory to God!*

The word submit is in very close relation to these two words, but again, we have to know where the word was first mentioned; in order to understand how God intended for the word to be used. Submit is recorded for the first time in Genesis 16:9, which says,

> *"The angel of the Lord said to her, 'Return to your mistress, and submit yourself under her hand."*

Submit here is derived from the Hebrew word *anah*, which means *to depress, abase self, afflict (-ion, self), answer, chasten self, deal hardly with, defile, exercise, force, gentleness, humble (self), hurt, ravish, submit self or weaken*. This word in Genesis 16:9 was spoken to Hagar, Sarai's maid, by the angel of the Lord. The angel told her to return to Sarai and submit herself *under* Sarai's hand.

Why would the angel of the Lord tell Hagar to do this? The Holy Spirit took me back to verse 2 where Sarai asked Abram to go into Hagar and possibly bear her children. It says that Abram heeded the voice of Sarai. This scripture is cross-referenced back to Genesis 3:17.

> *"Then to Adam He said, 'Because you have heeded the voice of your wife, and have eaten from the tree of which I commanded you saying, "You shall not eat of it": cursed is the ground for thy sake: in toil you shall eat of it all the days of your life."*

Neither Adam, nor Abram exercised their roles as husbands. They both heeded the voice of their unsubmissive wives, which led to judgment in the end. God could have let Hagar leave, but because of Abram's disobedience, like Adam's, he reaped what he sowed. Hagar was not exactly an innocent party in this confusion, but God extended His mercy to her. He told her to go back to Sarai and submit herself under her. Most people would have caught an attitude and left, but Hagar heard a Word from God and knew that He had a plan for her and her son, Ishmael.

Submission in this scripture deals with accepting the wrong that we do and receiving a just answer, or punishment, for it. This word is non-existent, until after the fall of man. We should assume that because man was created in the image of God, submission should not have even been an issue. Not until sin entered the world did God see fit for us to submit.

Adam and Eve were given dominion over all of the creatures and commanded to subdue the earth. There is no distinction of authority between Adam and Eve, until Genesis 3:16. God tells Eve that she will desire her husband and he will rule over her. There must have been an unseen, mutual understanding between Adam and Eve. Their union must have been peaceful and full of joy, as they had the earth under their authority.

We need submission in our lives to guard us from the tricks and schemes of the enemy. It brings order and purpose to everything and everyone in this world.

"Therefore submit to God, Resist the devil and he will flee from you." (James 4:7)

God guarantees that if we submit to Him; obey Him and resist the devil; stand against him and oppose him that he WILL flee from us. Submission is necessary in such an unstable world that we are living in today. Everyone wants to do things their own way. They say, *"If I can just become my own boss, I will not have to answer to anyone."* Oh, the devil is a LIAR! We all have to answer to God, so we need to submit now, so that we will not have to answer for it later.

We all need someone to hold us accountable for our actions. We need someone who can love us enough to tell us when we have fallen back. In Ephesians 5:21, Paul says to the church in Ephesus that you should be, *"submitting to one another in the fear of God."* Submitting here is in reference to a believer holding another believer accountable when we fall short. We need one another in this walk with God, so we should not resist submitting to our brothers and sisters in the Lord.

Again, submission is a very touchy subject for many people. I am here to let you know that the enemy has won a few battles in this area, because he has convinced us that we do not have to answer to anyone but ourselves. We have to empower ourselves by studying the Word of God and meditating daily on certain words and scriptures to find out how God sees them.

> *"My people are destroyed for a lack of knowledge. Because you have rejected knowledge, I will also reject you from being priest for Me; Because you have forgotten the law of your God, I will also forget your children." (Hosea 4:6)*

Satan knows that when we truly commit ourselves to reading God's Word daily and understanding the knowledge that it gives us, he is *FINISHED!* This is how he distracts us by keeping the focus on our own selfish desires, as opposed to keeping the focus on Jesus.

Do we want our children to suffer because we chose to ignore, or reject the knowledge of God? People, this is bigger than just our present situations. Our children and generations of children to come will bear the burden of our disobedience and unwillingness to submit. I believe the major component in successfully being able to submit is to *humble* ourselves. The word humble is defined as *being marked by meekness or modesty in behavior, attitude, or spirit*; *not arrogant or prideful*; *submissive respect*. The word humble is used for the first time in Exodus 10:3, which says,

> *"So Moses and Aaron came in to Pharaoh and said to him, 'Thus says the Lord God of the Hebrews, "How long will you*

> *refuse to humble yourself before me? Let my people go, that they may serve me."*

This is such a powerful use of the word humble. He said how long will you *REFUSE* to humble yourself? This is what we do. We refuse to humble ourselves for a moment in time, so that we may benefit further down the road. We want everything now and do not count the costs for ourselves or for our future generations. We are not promised tomorrow, but there is a promise for the generations to come.

> *"The haters of the Lord would pretend submission to Him, but their fate would endure forever." (Psalm 81:15)*

Do not allow the enemy to steal the promise for you or your children of eternal life with God. If we refuse to submit, then there is also a promise for us, but not one that we desire. Hagar humbled herself and went back to Sarai, as the angel of the Lord advised her to and submitted unto her, because she knew that there was a promise to her seed. God told her that He would make a nation for Ishmael, her son, and that his seed would be multiplied exceedingly. Hagar could have only thought of herself and allowed her pride to consume her, but she understood that this lesson was bigger than her current situation. This is Powerful! This was true humility and submission in the beginning; the first reference of submission in the Bible, and look at the reward that Hagar received, and she was not even included in the Promise, but the outsider. *Glory to God!* How much more are we to receive, being the sons of God?

Let us learn from her example and submit ourselves now, the temporary, so we may reap that which is eternal. *Glory to God!*

Prayer for Submission

Dear Heavenly Father, I pray that the Light of Your Word has exposed to us what true submission is in Your eyes and not what the world has made it out to be. I thank You that we are now equipped with the Truth, so that we can begin to walk in submission. Continue to guide us in this Truth by Your Holy Spirit. In Jesus' name. Amen.

Chapter 3
The Spirit of Pride

Pride is one of the most dangerous spirits that one can possess. It is so complex, because it has many branches that stem directly from it. Throughout this chapter, you will be exposed to these *"branches"*, and you will be able to recognize if this spirit of pride dwells on the inside of you.

> *"The fear of the Lord is to hate evil; pride and arrogance and the evil way and the perverse mouth I hate." (Proverbs 8:13)*

God hates pride. There is no way around it. This word pride is defined as *a sense of one's own proper dignity or value; self-respect; pleasure or satisfaction taken in an achievement, possession or association; arrogant or disdainful conduct or treatment, haughtiness or excessively high opinion of oneself; conceit.* This word is derived from several Hebrew words, but the one that suits this text is *ga'avah*, which means *arrogance or majesty; ornament; excellency, haughtiness, highness, pride, proud or swelling.*

This word screams out the *"I"* syndrome. *"I"* will do what *"I"* want to do. *"I"* know what is best for me. *"I"* am a grown man, or woman. *"I"* want this, *"I"* want that, *"I"* deserve to have the best. God is getting tired of hearing *"I"* from us people. We are selfish people with selfish desires, the *"Eve Mentality"*. We want God to answer our prayers as quickly as they leave our mouths. We expect Him to move on our behalf, but what we fail to realize is that if pride dwells in us, we are not in relationship with our Father.

> *"You ask and do not receive because you ask amiss, that you many spend it on your good pleasures."(James 4:3)*

We cannot expect God to bless us when we are acting in this manner. We get so puffed up within ourselves that we think the world owes us something and we ask God to give it to us. How do we sound? We are asking God to give us something that the world owes us. We are contradicting ourselves.

> *"Whoever therefore wants to be a friend of this world, makes himself and enemy of God."(James 4:4)*

We see here that God says He will have nothing to do with those who seek worldly gain of any sort. He calls you His enemy! That puts you right in line behind satan, or better yet, right beside him. Is this the way that you want God to see you? Do you want God to hear your prayers and answer them? Do you want your Father to protect you from the evils of this world?

> *"But He gives more grace. Therefore He says, 'God resists the proud, but gives grace to the humble."(James 4:6)*

Humble yourselves under the mighty hand of God and allow Him to purge this spirit from you. We have to see that there is only one way to approach the Father and that is through humbling ourselves and acknowledging that He is Lord and that we are but flesh. The more that we try to approach the Father with a non-chalant attitude the more we will suffer.

Nothing that you have tried so far is working, so try something new; learn to humble yourself and seek the Father. In his autobiography, Benjamin Franklin spoke on pride and humility and it was a great example of how we should tackle pride in our lives. It shows us that humility is the only way to conquer pride. It says:

"There is perhaps no one of our natural passions so hard to subdue as pride. Beat it down, stifle it, mortify it as much as one pleases, it is still alive. Even if I could conceive that I had completely overcome it, I should probably be proud of my humility." Benjamin Franklin

The Controlling Spirit

Pride manifests itself in many different ways, one being control. Many of us, at one point in our lives, possessed a controlling spirit. There is always something that we refuse to give up in this world. We can coin these as our own *"hang-ups"*. Some will use the phrase, *"This is just how I am and I will not change for anyone"*. This is pride. Anything that we are not willing to give up or change about ourselves is in essence, controlling something that no one else can. There is power in this type of control, because no one can make you change, not even God. He gives us free will to choose how we want to live our lives, but He also gives us many warnings about holding pride in our hearts.

"Pride goes before destruction, and a haughty spirit before a fall."(Proverbs 16:18)

People that possess pride in themselves look as if they have it all together on the outside, but are truly unhappy on the inside. God said that these people will fall with this type of spirit. Nothing good comes from pride, especially a controlling spirit. We try to control every aspect of our lives from whom we want to marry, to when we want to have children. What we fail to realize is that God is in control of *ALL* of this. Even if you think that you made the decision, He already made it before you were even born. *GLORY TO GOD!* He may not stop us when we make a stupid decision, but He is always in control.

> *"Since his days are determined, The number of months is with You; You have appointed his limits, so that he cannot pass." (Job 14:5)*

Please do not allow the enemy to trick you into believing that having control is a good thing. He is a LIAR! Allow yourself the opportunity to become humbled before the Lord and watch Him elevate you in due time.

The Selfish Spirit

Many times, we find ourselves in a position where we are only thinking of what we want. We refuse to give up some things in this life, because they give us status or a position in society. We work so hard to build a *"name"* for ourselves that we cannot allow others to see us *"naked"*, if you will. We build a huge wall around us and orchestrate a certain *"lifestyle"* that we try to constantly keep up with to please others. My friend, while you are trying to keep up with the *"Jones"*, they are leading you straight to hell.

> *"not a novice, lest being puffed up with pride he fall into the same condemnation as the devil." (1Timothy 3:6)*

Pride was the root of satan's fall. He was selfish. He wanted a position that was only God's to have, and he used his cunningness to sway Eve away with this very same desire to have wisdom as God did.

We refuse to allow God to guide us in our ordained purposes for our lives, mostly because of our *"idols"* that we refuse to give up. For unbelievers, this is just what they do, but for "believers" this is very dangerous. We profess to be Christians, following after the teachings of Christ, but we conveniently skip the ones that will expose us for what we really are. I looked up the word convenience and it is defined as *the quality of being suitable to one's comfort, purposes or needs.* This is how we are seeking God! We want Him to bless us to suit our own comfort, purposes, and needs when we should be seeking His purpose for our lives.

> *"Will you steal, murder, commit adultery, swear falsely, burn incense to Baal, and walk after other gods whom you do not know", (verse 10) "and then come and stand before Me in this house which is called by My Name, and say, 'We are delivered to do all these abominations?"(Jeremiah 7:9-10)*

God is speaking to Christians here, not unbelievers. These people come into the house of the Lord to worship, but have hidden sin and agendas in their hearts. We have to realize that nothing is hidden from the face of God. He is the *"Omniscient"* God; He sees everything. *Nothing* is hidden from Him. This is one of the worst forms of pride, because we are lying to God. We truly believe that we can fool God, but He is not moved by our ignorance. He warns us repeatedly to remove pride from our hearts, but we choose not to. We cannot as Christians, decide how to live our own lives, because we gave up that right when we gave it over to God. A Christian is one who follows Christ. He gave up His own will, His own life, for us so, that we could live in eternity with God. Why are we so selfish that we cannot give up our *"foolishness"* to serve Him? *Glory to God!*

Pride is an ugly thing people. We have to examine ourselves and make sure that it does not manifest in our lives in the form of *selfishness*.

The Unforgiving Spirit

Another *"branch"* of pride is unforgiveness. When we choose not to forgive someone, it is just that, "a choice". As we saw from the controlling spirit and the selfish spirit, we have a choice to decide to live in this manner. This is how satan wants us to live, with more choices than we have time to make them.

Forgiving someone takes a great deal of selflessness. It is saying, *"No matter what you do, I choose to suppress my pride, humble myself and acknowledge that we are all imperfect people"*. Forgiveness is saying, *"I am willing to sacrifice my feelings for the release of someone else's burden of guilt"*. There is power in forgiveness and the enemy knows it. This is why he tries to hold us in bondage, sometimes even for a lifetime. He makes us feel like we are the one that deserves an apology and that we should not be the one to extend the forgiveness. He confuses us so much with pride that even if someone does ask us to forgive them, we either say we forgive them and do not really mean it, or we just outright choose not to forgive at all. This is not of God!

> *"But if you do not forgive men their trespasses, neither will your Father forgive your trespasses." (Matthew 6:15)*

The other side of this is in us asking someone else to forgive us for the wrong that we have done. This is much harder to do than the former. Now we have to expose ourselves for what we have done. Satan desires for us to stay in this position. As long as we are suffering in guilt, or sin, he is happy. He tries to keep us in this state as long as he can, so that we become so enslaved by it that we see no hope for another's forgiveness, let alone God's, but there is hope my friend.

> *"to open their eyes, in order to turn them from darkness to light, and from the power of Satan to God, that they may receive forgiveness of sins and an inheritance among those who are sanctified by faith in Me." (Acts 26:18)*

Satan is trying to blind us through these many forms of pride, so that we do not see the real Truth of Jesus Christ. This is the whole reason that Christ died for us. He died so that we may live eternally.

> *"If we confess our sins, He is faithful and just to forgive us our sins and to cleanse us from all unrighteousness."(1 John 1:9)*

Do not be afraid to confess your wrongdoings to others or your sins to God. You are a child of God, and He will forgive you *EVERY* time.

Shame

Unforgiveness, if not dealt with, can lead to shame, another one of the *" branches"* of pride. Shame is defined as *a painful emotion caused by a strong sense of guilt, embarrassment, unworthiness, or disgrace*. Whatever the root of the issue is in your life that you feel you cannot share with others, it is not too big for God. Satan would have us to believe this, but it is absolutely not true. God's desire is for us to confess our sins, so that we may be forgiven and released from that guilt, not for it to burden us.

> *"For I will be merciful to their unrighteousness and their sins and their lawless deeds and I will remember them no more." (Hebrews 8:12)*

God is merciful. He did not send His only Son to die for us and then decide not to forgive us when we ask. This contradicts the whole purpose of Jesus' death. You should not be so ashamed of your problems that you cannot release them. We all have problems in this life; how you handle them will determine your outcome.

There are times when we can become so puffed up that we feel we do not have to answer to anyone. Proverbs 11:2 describes this type of person very well. It says,

> *"When pride cometh, then cometh shame, but with the lowly is wisdom."*

Do not fool yourself into believing that you are happy, when pride is destroying your life. It will always lead to shame, because you know in your spirit (inner man) that you are wrong and this will haunt you, until you make it right. There are times when pride creeps in without us knowing, but there will be shame that follows, so you will be able to recognize it when it comes. Many times it comes because either our families before us have sinned against God or we have ourselves. We have to understand that our decisions in this life have consequences and we cannot hide from them.

> *"We lie down in our shame, and our reproach covers us. For we have sinned against the Lord our God, we and our fathers, from our youth even to this day. And have not obeyed the voice of the Lord our God."(Jeremiah 3:25)*

This, again, is a choice people. You have the power within to choose life, instead of death. If you want to continue living the way you have been, then that is your choice, but I am here to tell you that pride will destroy your life if you do. It consumed me and I was not even aware that it was there, until someone revealed it to me. I finally understood why my situation was not changing, why my life was at a standstill, and why my marriage was suffering.

Again, pride is like cancer, it will spread quickly if it is not caught early on, and shame will definitely be one of the *"branches"* that you will notice develop in your life because of it.

Strife

We have seen that pride breeds many different kinds of *"branches"*. Another one of the stems of pride is strife. This word is defined as *a heated, often violent dissension; bitter conflict.* This type of behavior can be summed up briefly, as *confusion.* Strife is a result of shame. As we saw previously, shame results from not confessing our wrongs, because we do not want to be exposed to others. As we continue on this destructive path, we become angry and contentious, because we do not know what else to do. It could begin with an outburst of anger, triggered by something that you have been holding back. You become uncomfortable, because you do not want to confront this issue. It has made you remember the problem, and now it is right in your face again.

Satan thrives on this type of "cancer". Unlike physical cancer, pride and it's *"branches"* can live on in us for a very long time unnoticed, without any real signs. He desires for these behaviors to progress, so that they will consume us, causing us to die in our sin, ultimately to spend eternity in hell with him. God tells us something different in the Word.

> *"Hatred stirs up strife, but love covers all sins."*
> *(Proverbs 10:12)*

The only way for us to see this love in the midst of our trials is to give everything over to God and trust Him to give us peace. We have to know what His Word promises us. We have to have confidence in Him, that whatever His Word says, is true.

> *"He who is of a proud heart stirs up strife, but he who trusts in the Lord will be prospered." (Proverbs 28:25)*

The progression of these spirits causes us to go deeper into hopelessness. We have to recognize them for what they are and defeat them before they envelop our lives. Satan loves to see God's people in confusion, and we know that God is not the author of it. He pulls us in so many different directions that we cannot see straight. This is how the spirits metamorphose, through confusion, and that is why satan tries to keep us in the darkness as long as he can.

"For where envying and strife is, there is confusion and every evil work." (James 3:16, KJV)

Therefore, recognize these spirits and catch them early on before they progress into this type of behavior.

The Danger of Isolation

The many different *"branches"* that we saw in pride were: control, selfishness, unforgiveness, shame, and strife. There are many different spirits that can form from pride. These are the ones that the Holy Spirit revealed to me when writing this text. The last one that I will touch on is *isolation*. From the beginning of creation, satan has tried to isolate us from our true purpose in life. He led Eve astray by isolating her from Adam, her head, causing her to disobey God's command. Adam was also isolated from God in relationship, because of his role in the disobedience. Satan's ultimate goal is to isolate us all from the love of God by keeping us so bound in sin that we do not recognize how powerful our Father is to deliver us out of it.

The word isolate is defined as *to set apart or cut off from others; solitary or alone*. This word is non-existent in the Bible, but the word alone is used and it is derived from the Hebrew word *bad*, which means *to separate, apart, only, besides, branch, by self, except and only*. This is how satan desires to get us; alone, so he can put his thoughts in our head and try to deceive us.

> *"And the Lord God said, 'It is not good that man should be alone; I will make him a helper comparable to him."(Genesis 2:18)*

If God said it is not good to be alone, then we need to find out why it is not, so that we can be empowered against the tricks of the enemy.

> *"Lest Satan should take advantage of us; for we are not ignorant of his devices." (2 Corinthians 2:11)*

We have to know who the enemy is and how he operates, so that we do not fall into his trap of isolating us. The word ignorant is defined as *lacking education or knowledge; unaware or uninformed*. This word is derived from the Greek word *agnoeo*, which means *not to know, not understand, or unknown*. God has not left us out there to the enemy. He has given us His Word as a weapon against the wiles of the devil.

We can isolate ourselves in many ways, one being in marriage. We saw from Genesis that satan wanted to destroy the union of marriage. He understood that when God said that they would be one flesh, he was finished, but he still pursued his plan by isolating Eve from Adam. This is how he wants the married couple to be. He wants to confuse our roles to the point where we no longer want to be around our spouses. This is a very dangerous place to be, because this is how he tempts us to sin.

> *"Do not deprive one another except with consent for a time, that you may give yourselves to fasting and prayer and come together again so that Satan does not tempt you because of your lack of self-control."(1 Corinthians 7:5)*

This is a major reason that God would not have us to isolate ourselves in marriage. Most often, we get into heated discussions with our spouses and one will end up sleeping on the couch or in another room. Other times, without even noticing it, we separate ourselves by falling into the enemy's trap of telling us that we need time to ourselves. I am here to tell you that the devil is a LIAR!

> *"Be sober, be vigilant; because your adversary the devil walks about like a roaring lion, seeking whom he may devour."(1 Peter 5:8)*

There are many times throughout our day when we have time to be alone, but be aware that the enemy knows how long it will take to tempt you. He wants us to find hobbies or interests that our spouses do not like, so that he can keep us from them as long as he possibly can, to tempt us. We fall into this trap and begin to tell our spouses that we no longer have anything in common with them, which can lead to us looking elsewhere for someone who does. Catch this people! The devil is playing us like a puppet and we are too blind to see it!

We have to recognize how these spirits come into operation. Remember, isolation is a result of pride. We isolate ourselves, because we refuse to confront the issues surrounding our lives. Instead of facing them head on, we suppress our feelings and go into our caves. We refuse to admit that they even exist, and when a situation arises to bring that issue back up, we get defensive and again, try to conceal it. This is not of God, but of the enemy.

> *"We are of God, he who knows God hears us; he who is not of God does not hear us. By this we know the spirit of truth and the spirit of error."(1 John 4:6)*

If we continue to live in isolation and ignore the spirit of truth, our marriages will be in danger. We have to break this spirit and submit to the leading of the Holy Spirit.

Next, we can isolate ourselves by not fellowshipping with other people. Just like in marriage, we feel that we have nothing in common with other couples. Instead of introducing yourself to someone else, you continue to live your routine life and this can lead to depression. The enemy does not want us to connect with other believers, because he knows that this is how God builds us up, through fellowship. When we connect with other believers, we expose ourselves to other people who are just as *imperfect* as we are. This gives us a sense of relief that we are not the only ones going through these issues.

> *"not forsaking the assembling of ourselves together, as in the manner of some, but exhorting one another, and so much more as you see the Day approaching." (Hebrews 10:25)*

God understood the need for fellowship amongst the believers. He knows the plots and schemes that satan uses to distract us, so He gives us a way to defeat it, by fellowshipping with our brothers and sisters. Make it a point to invite your *"family"* over, because they too may be feeling the same way that you are, *"We do not have anything in common with them."* You would be surprised at how much you do have in common with them. Satan wants to keep you apart, because he knows this. The very situation you are going through may very well be the same that your brother or sister is going through. God sends you in the path of a person for a reason. He knows what you need to make it through a situation, and who will help you through it.

> *"Bear one another's burdens, and so fulfill the law of Christ." (Galatians 6:2)*

Just as Jesus bore our burdens on the cross, we should bear the burdens of our brothers and sisters to encourage and lift them up. We need each other people. We need others to stand in agreement with us and pray with us so that the enemy cannot tempt us. He gets us alone, so that we have no other example of deliverance to see. Our problems become so overwhelming that when we look to God for help, we feel so unworthy because of our sin that we feel He is too holy to answer such a filthy person. Well God is, but He sent His Son Jesus to bridge the gap for us. God desires for us to connect with other believers who are like us, *imperfect*.

> *"Confess your trespasses to one another, and pray for one another that you may be healed. The effective, fervent prayer of a righteous man avails much."(James 5:16)*

When we have someone who understands what we are going through and have come out of the same situation, it gives us comfort and encouragement. This is His desire for us. He not only gave us His Son, but other believers to hold us up when we cannot hold ourselves up.

Another way that we isolate ourselves is by not attending a local church. Many people believe that they do not have to go to church to believe in God. How can we believe in God if we do not know who He is? We have to be a part of a church to be able to hear the Word of God on a consistent basis.

> *"How then shall they call on Him in whom they have not believed? And how shall they believe in Him of whom they have not heard? And how shall they hear without a preacher? (Romans 10:14)*

You cannot know God without having a man or woman of God who is teaching and preaching the Word of God. Revelation comes to our shepherds from the Holy Spirit in reference to our lives. God places them over us to teach us and guide us in our spiritual walk. So, do not let satan tell you that you do not have to go to church to be saved. He does not even try to tell you that you are not saved. He just tries to keep you as far away from the Word and the Spirit as possible, so that you will not know the difference. He knows that when you are connected to a church where the Word is being taught, you will know the *real* from the *fake*.

> *"So they rose early in the morning and went out into the wilderness of Tekoa; and as they went out, Jehoshaphat stood and said, 'Believe in the Lord your God and you shall be established; believe His prophets, and you shall succeed."(2 Corinthians 20:20)*

The devil does not want us to catch this revelation, so he tries every trick in his power, *which is limited*, to deceive us. The further that we are from church, the more isolated we are from God. This is satan's ultimate desire for believers. No matter how he tries to isolate us, it ultimately leads to the separation of us from the love of God. We have to empower ourselves and be ready to stand and defend our belief in God and His Son Jesus Christ. Surround yourself with believers of *"like faith"* and connect to a house of God that is teaching the Word, where you can be taught the doctrine of Christ, as well as the devices of satan, so you can have the armor you need to defeat the enemy. *You will prevail!*

The Spirit of Rebellion/Witchcraft

We look back at all of the spirits that we have discussed so far and understand that they all are bad, but the danger of them all is what we *do not* see. Rebellion is defined as *an act or a show of defiance toward an authority or established convention*. This word is derived from the Hebrew word *meriy*, which means *bitterness; rebellious*, or *marah*, which means *change, disobey, grievously, provocation, or provoke; to rebel against*. What we fail to realize from these different spirits is that we are operating in rebellion. Through control, selfishness, unforgiveness, shame, strife, and even isolation, we are behaving in a defiant manner. Defiant is defined as *boldly resisting*. Listen to that! We are not only resisting, but also doing it with an *ATTITUDE!*

This is a very dangerous position to be in people. Again, this is saying, *"I am grown"*, *"I am my own person"*, *"I am going to do it whether you like it or not"*. Operating in this way of life draws us closer into satan's trap with each new progression of spirit.

> *"An evil man seeks only rebellion; therefore a cruel messenger will be sent against him."(Proverbs 17:11)*

God tells us here that there will be severe punishment for dealing in rebellion. Satan wants us to believe that we have complete control over our lives and there are no real consequences for our disobedience. He puffs up the pride in us to a point where we feel we are untouchable, but I am here to tell you that there is judgment awaiting you if you do not turn from rebellion.

Witchcraft is defined as *magic or the art of sorcery.* This word is derived from the Hebrew word *qecem,* which means *a lot, an oracle, or a divine sentence.* The word lot is the Hebrew word *goral,* which means *portion or destiny.* Why am I giving you the definition of witchcraft? I am glad that you asked. Many of us are not aware of the hidden dangers of pride; those things that God sees in the Spirit. As we are operating in rebellion, the different spirits are in operation themselves. One of the definitions of witchcraft was sorcery. Sorcery is defined as *the use of supernatural powers over others through the assistance of spirits; witchcraft.*

Did you catch that? We are operating in the supernatural, not with God, but with satan. Satan also possesses supernatural abilities and uses them to trick us. Through the assistance of the different spirits that we spoke of earlier, we are operating in witchcraft. I know that this may be hard for some of you to believe, but it is the truth, the Word of God says it.

> *"For rebellion is as the sin of witchcraft, and stubbornness is as iniquity and idolatry, because you have rejected the Word of the Lord, He has also rejected you from being king."(1 Samuel 15:23)*

God will reject us if we operate in this type of behavior. Do not believe that this one little spirit, whether it is control or unforgiveness is not harmful, because God says it is. We know that the more mess that we get ourselves into, the harder it is for us to get out. We do not end up with what we started with, because there was no exposing of the culprit from the beginning.

> *"Your glorying is not good. Do you not know that a little leaven leavens the whole lump."(1 Corinthians 5:6)*

One spirit in you that is not of God can cause Him to reject you completely. It is that simple! We have to gain knowledge through the Word of God concerning how these spirits come about and how they operate. When we come into the knowledge, it will be easier to recognize if a spirit is trying to attach itself to us. Please do not think that if you have possessed or still do possess one or more of these spirits that there is no hope for you, because the Word says something different.

> *"They refused to obey, and they were not mindful of your wonders that you did among them, but they hardened their necks, and in their rebellion they appointed a leader to return to their bondage, but you are God. Ready to pardon, gracious and merciful, slow to anger, abundant in kindness and did not forsake them."(Nehemiah 9:17)*

GLORY TO GOD! God always gives us a way of escape! No matter whom you were or what you used to do, or even do in the future, God says He will pardon us our sins if we just ask Him.

We saw that witchcraft is the Hebrew *quecem*, which means *a lot, an oracle, or a divine sentence*. Lot is the Hebrew *goral*, which means *portion or destiny*. There are only two choices in this life: *good or evil*? You can choose your divine sentence in *Heaven or Hell*? You can choose your portion in *Heaven or Hell*? The choice is *Yours*! What choice will you make today?

Prayer against Pride

Father, I come to Your throne of grace through the name of Your Son Jesus Christ and ask that You empower every believer who is reading this book. Allow Your Holy Spirit to reveal specifically, by name, every spirit that may be in operation in our lives that are holding us back from receiving all that You have for us. We come up against and bind that ugly spirit of pride and all of the *"branches"* that stem from it and release the Spirit of Truth and humility into our lives. We thank You for burdens being removed, yokes being destroyed, chains being loosed, and souls set free as we open up our eyes, our ears, and our hearts entirely to receive the Word from You. In Jesus' name. Amen.

Chapter 4
Submission in the Marriage: "The Role of the Woman"

We will start with the role of the woman in marriage, because we found from Genesis 3:6 that Eve was the first to eat of the tree of the knowledge of good and evil. What I have truly come to realize from the intimate time of fellowship that I have had with the Holy Spirit in writing this book, is that I am accountable for myself only, not my husband. I do not have time to worry about what "I think" he is doing wrong, because the Holy Spirit revealed to me a *"Mountain"* of wrongs in my own life that needed to be changed.

I pray that you will humble yourself and allow the Spirit to minister to your specific situation. Many of these situations may not apply to you, but the Word of God applies to us all. If they do apply, then I have to let you know that I cannot apologize for the boldness in these words. The Holy Spirit revealed to me that it was *necessary* that a certain tone be set forth in this book concerning submission, so it can break the chains of bondage from our marriages. If you are tired of the enemy's schemes to destroy your family, as I am, then sit back and receive what the Spirit is saying to you.

The Role of the Wife

Women, stop trying to fix your husbands, because you *CANNOT!* As women, we believe that we know what is best for our husbands when in reality we have *NO CLUE!* God created him, not you! Only the creator of a thing can know the purpose for which it was created. We are all created with a purpose, and life is about letting God use us for His purposes, not us using Him for our own personal gain. The same holds true for women. We were created for man, not man for us.

> *"Nor was man created for the woman, but woman for the man."(1 Corinthians 16:9)*

We try to use God, manipulate His greatness, in order to change our husband's minds. God is the only One who can change your husband and that is by His choosing, not yours!

Maybe your husband is not the one who needs to change, but you. We are always telling them that something is wrong with them and asking them, or telling them, *"If only you would let God change you?"* My God! Do we really hear ourselves when we talk to, or better yet, at our husbands? We do not have a clue! Matthew 7:1-6 is a wonderful example of why we should not confront others to change. Verse 5 says,

> *"Hypocrite! First remove the plank from your eye, and then you will see clearly to remove the speck from your brother's eye."*

When we first meet our prospective spouses, we fall so head over heels in love with them that we do not evaluate what it is that we are expecting from them. I can guarantee that you did not fall in love, but into *LUST* with him. Look back at Genesis 3:6 which says,

> *"So when the woman saw that the tree was good for food, that it was pleasant to the eyes, and a tree desirable to make one wise, she took of its fruit and ate."*

Again, Eve saw with her eyes something that was good and she took of it. This is how we fall into lust so easily. We see what we think is good, as opposed to what we know is right. We become so blinded by this lust that we forget to ask all the pertinent questions needed to know our perspective mate. We are so high up in the clouds that we refuse to listen to the advice of those around us who are thinking rationally. Before we know it we are married, either by naivety or because we allowed our lust to produce a child.

Now you want to change the brother. You all of a sudden decide that there is something wrong with him now that the ring is on the finger and the papers are signed! *Ladies, analyze you!* Who are you to say that your husband needs to change? You chose him! You made the decision to spend the rest of your life with this man and because you chose him, you have to deal with everything about him.

> *"For my thoughts are not your thoughts, nor are your ways My ways", says the Lord. "For as the heavens are higher than the earth, so are My ways higher than your ways, and My thoughts than your thoughts." (Isaiah 55:8-9)*

God created your husband with a purpose and you cannot change that purpose to suit your needs. Who are you to decide what is best for him? God is the only One that can reveal His plans for your husband and when He does, He *WILL NOT* reveal it to you! So stop lying to your husband, as well as yourself, by telling him what the Holy Spirit revealed to you about him. This is *NOT* how God operates.

There are times when the Holy Spirit may reveal something to you about your husband, or even about the part *YOU* play in it, but this will happen only if you are submitting to your head.

> *"Beloved, do not believe every spirit, but test the spirits, whether they are of God; because many false prophets have gone out into the world."(1 John 4:1)*

God would not reveal your husbands purpose to you, because you cannot even handle your own purpose, let alone his. You are too *BUSY* worrying about what you think he should be doing that you lose sight of your purpose in this marriage. Women let us admit it! We are governed by our emotions.

> *"And the Lord caused a deep sleep to fall on Adam, and he slept; and He took one of his ribs, and closed up the flesh in its place." (Verse 22) "Then the rib which the Lord God had taken from man He made into a woman, and He brought her to Adam."(Genesis 2:21-22)*

We are not given a specific proximity of where the rib was taken, but in my *"spiritual imagination"*, I see it taken from over Adam's heart. I say this, because the heart is the center of emotions.

> *"Keep your heart with all diligence, for out of it spring the issues of life."(Proverbs 4:23)*

Women do not usually make rational decisions, but emotional ones, because we allow our feelings to overrule or cloud our judgment. Even though some men do not express sensitivity as we do, they have the ability to think rationally and have decision-making capabilities far beyond what we *"see"*. If we women want our husbands to soar like eagles, set free, then we need to release the chains from them. I know that you have heard the saying *"the old ball and chain?"* I used to get so upset when I heard someone use this phrase to describe their wife, but this is truly how they feel when we are acting overbearing. Stop trying to change them, because you

CANNOT! Stop trying to fix things, because you are probably the one who messed it up! Stop trying to tell him who he is; you do not even know who you are! *GLORY TO GOD!*

Assume your position women and get out of his! Eve was created to compliment Adam, not to take his position, but she stepped out of her role and into his and made a life-altering decision. If we want to see our husbands reach their full, God-given potential that He created in them, then we need to step down, and out of their role as head of the family. We need to allow them to step up and make decisions for their families, even if we do not agree with it! We should assume our submissive roles as wives, under their authority, being the weaker vessel; respect it, admire it, want it, and thank God for it!

Do you realize how much stress it creates in a person when they take on situations that they have not been equipped to handle? God did not want us in this position. He knew that we would not prosper in this role. God created Adam with wisdom to govern all the creatures of the earth. Adam did not need more wisdom he needed companionship and co-rulership. God, in His infinite wisdom, would not create woman to rule over what He already created wise.

> *"For God is not the author of confusion, but of peace, as in all the churches of the saints."(1Corinthians 14:33)*

The confusion in our homes in not of God, but a result of us not knowing our strategic positioning in our marriages. Once we come under our husband's authority, not forcefully, but submissively, we will begin to see them grow and prosper like never before.

We have not allowed our husbands to be men, because we are treating them like our children. We have failed to fulfill our role as their companion by not lifting them up and encouraging them for being the men that God created them to be. Instead, we have criticized them, put them down, and trampled on their egos. This is not by any means a way to make women feel bad for every wrong decision made in their home or for every trial that their husbands face. This is not your fault, nor can you fix it for them, but stand by them and support them, as they make the family decisions. Stand back and ask yourselves, *"How long will my husband have to go through these trials because of my attitude towards him, as well as towards God?"*

God allows us to go through trials to test and build our character. He is doing a perfect work in you, as well as your husband; in His way and in His timing.

> *"The Lord is in His holy temple, the Lord's throne is in heaven; His eyes behold, His eyelids test the sons of men. The Lord tests the righteous, but the wicked and the one who loves violence His soul hates."(Psalm 11:4)*

Ladies, stand back and allow God to do His job and stop trying to do it for Him. The more you antagonize your husband and keep strife in your household shows that you are the *ONE* who loves violence and God hates this. Do not let yourself be the *ONE* that receives judgment from the Lord.

Meanwhile, find out what your role in this marriage is supposed to be. Seek God and ask His forgiveness for your part in the breaking down of your marriage. Ask Him to reveal His purpose for your life. Even though we are married, we have an individual walk with the Lord. You cannot save him nor can he save you. Our husbands do need us; this was made clear in the Word of God.

> *"It is not good that man should be alone; I will make him a helper comparable to him."(Genesis 2:18)*

This word helper in the Hebrew is *ezer*, which means *to aid*. The word aid is defined as *help, support, relief, or assistance*. Therefore, we have to understand that, as wives, we hold only a supporting role in the marriage, not the major role. This may be hard for many of you to accept, but if you are truly tired of the confusion in your marriage, as I am, you will accept it, receive it, and change it.

Without a good woman, a submissive woman, who prays and intercedes on behalf of her husband, without stepping into his role, he cannot be the man that God created him to be. So, even though we hold a supporting role, it is a major role to God. He foreknew the impact that we would have in our husband's lives. We were made to compliment him, not control him. Again, we are very sensitive and emotional beings. Some may view these attributes as weak, but I have to disagree. I see them as strengths in regards to prayer and intercession. Women, we could do damage to the enemy if we would only take the anger that we have been inflicting on our husbands and use it on satan! Go into warfare for your husband and your family!

> *"For we do not wrestle against flesh and blood, but against principalities, against powers, against the rulers of the darkness of this age, against spiritual hosts of wickedness in the heavenly places."(Ephesians 6:12)*

Ladies, you are not fighting against your husbands, you are battling against wickedness in the spiritual realm; satan and his demons. He is sending these demons to distract you and to tear your family apart. If you are now convinced that the enemy has had his hand in your marriage, then you need to be empowered on how to do *YOUR* part to get him out.

The enemy's agenda is to twist the Truth and deceive us by showing us a picture of perfection. There is no perfect marriage or perfect life here on earth. Satan tries to show us this picture, so that we will do everything we can to get it, even leaving our partners in search of it. The enemy even tried to tempt our Lord by showing Him a picture of what he called a "perfect" life.

> *"Then the devil, taking Him up on a high mountain, showed Him all the kingdoms of the world in a moment of time."(Luke 4:5)*

Satan tried to tempt Jesus into believing that he could give Him authority, but in verse 8 it says,

> *"And Jesus answered him and said to him, 'Get behind Me Satan!'"(Luke 4:8)*

We should be exercising the authority that God gave to us, by putting satan and his schemes behind us and moving on. The devil is a LIAR! Do not give place to him that he may tempt you. We give satan more power than he actually has by just giving him an inch into our lives.

> *"Therefore submit to God, Resist the devil and he will flee from you."(James 4:7)*

This sounds simple and to the point in scripture, but we tend to make it more difficult, because of our *"Eve Mentality"*. We refuse to submit to our husbands, as well as God; therefore, allowing the enemy right in the door.

We will go through trials and tribulations in this life, but the test is how we handle them. They make us strong and allow us a peace when we encounter a new one. The enemy does not want us to catch this revelation. He tries to blind us into believing that if we can change our spouses, we will have the life that we desire. You will have the life that you desire as you humble yourself and submit, not only to your husband, but also to God.

<u>The Puzzle</u>

Are you a fit for your husband? As a wife, do you move freely in your position in the family or do you try to squeeze and push your way into one? If you are the right piece for the *"puzzle"*, then you should easily fit in. Man was not created for woman, but woman for man. (Genesis 2:18) You were made to be a blessing for him, not a curse. You were made to be his companion, not his mother. Therefore, instead of trying to fix him, which I believe we all agree that we cannot, be for him what was missing from him in the beginning. Be someone in whom he can share his blessings with; whom he can come to and share his most intimate secrets with, and not take away from him, but add to him.

> *"Then God said, 'Let us make man in Our image, according to Our likeness, let them have dominion over the fish of the sea, over the birds of the air, and over the cattle, over all the earth and every creeping thing that creeps on the earth."(Genesis 1:26)*

WOW! Our husbands have got it going on! Look at how God created them, in His image and His likeness and gave them dominion over the wild animals of the earth too! Our husbands are men of status, men of wisdom, and men of authority! This should make us get goose bumps all over ourselves! We have been praying for this kind of man ladies! What we fail to realize is that we already have him. God has given us these men and what we want to do is change them. Wake up women and stop allowing the enemy to deceive you. If you go down to verse 31 of Genesis Chapter 1, it says,

> *"Then God saw everything that He made, and indeed it was very good. So the evening and the morning were the sixth day."*

GLORY TO GOD! He did not say maybe, He did not say probably; He said *INDEED* that it was very *"good"*.

Therefore, God Almighty said that He created man and it was good. Who are we to say that our husbands, our men of God, are not good enough? If God created them and proclaimed that it was good, what right do you have to say that he is worthless or inadequate? God gave these men purpose in this earth and I believe that if it was not for us nagging and putting them down, they would be walking in their destined purposes right now. *GLORY TO GOD!* I know that this may be a hard pill to swallow, but if you really want a marriage made in heaven, you will humble yourself and receive it.

We are calling our husbands inadequate, when we are the ones who do not know where our place is. We have become the inadequate ones. Who has tried to fix what God said is good? Who has tried to assume a position that they were not created to have? Who has tried to make decisions that they are not equipped to handle, the *"Eve Mentality"*?

Women are making decisions for their families every day without even consulting with their husbands. We are taking the future of our families into our own hands and truly believing that it is going to be better. Oh, the devil is a LIAR! Satan is ripping apart our family's right before our very eyes and we are so blinded by selfishness that we cannot even see it. We are slowly destroying the seeds that God planted in our husbands.

> *"Just as He chose us in Him before the foundation of the world, that we should be holy and without blame before Him in love." (Ephesians 1:4)*

God chose your husband before the foundation of the world and gave him purpose. Every time that you tell him he is worthless, you begin to destroy confidence in him that God placed in him before you even came into the picture. *HALLELUJAH!*

> *"Before I formed you in the womb I knew you: Before you were born I sanctified you; I ordained you a prophet to the nations." (Jeremiah 1:5)*

God has promised your husband some things before he was formed in his mother's womb. Do not be the one to hinder that process for your husband. You will be even more unsatisfied with him if you continue to act in this manner. Men do not change overnight and some will not ever change if you continue to hassle them. We try to step over our husbands by any means necessary, and that includes withholding of sex, because we are not getting what we want. We are stripping them of their manhood, trampling on their egos, and choking their purpose right out of them. We are causing our husbands to question their manhood ladies; not only their ability to be a good husband, but to question himself as a man of God. What could be worse for a man?

I was quickened in my spirit concerning this type of behavior and the Holy Spirit revealed that because we are administering this emotional abuse to our husbands, this is not only why they step out of marriage with other women, but more often than we know it, with men. I know this may be hard for many to believe, or talk about, but it is real. When men commit adultery, the majority of the time it is because their wives withhold themselves sexually from their husbands.

> *"Do not deprive one another except for consent for a time, that you may give yourselves to fasting and prayer; and come together again so that Satan does not tempt you because of your lack of self control."(1 Corinthians 7:5)*

God clearly states that adultery will take place if we deprive one another of sexual gratification. You cannot manipulate your husband by not having sex with him, because I can guarantee you that it will backfire on you. We manipulate our partners because we are not getting what we want or think we deserve. This is not of God, but of satan. We have to understand one another better and we do this by communicating with one another.

Men need to know, need to hear from their wives, that they are *kings* in their homes. They desire to be able to supply all of the needs of the family and have them lack for nothing. This is not always the case, so their wives may need *to support* them to meet the family's needs. We still need to reassure them that they are *kings*. We cannot take this opportunity to usurp authority in any way, because we are *supporting* our man of God, not taking over.

What I have seen from homosexual couples is that there is a definite *"male"* role and a definite *"female"* role. Most men in these relationships that bear the *"female"* role boost the egos of the other mate tremendously. They make them feel as if they hold real purpose in the relationship. His ego is being fed daily, so this allows him a sense of accomplishment in his life. He is being fulfilled emotionally, so whatever else comes, he is built up as a man. Men can cheat with women daily and still be unfulfilled, because they are seeking purpose and they will find it somewhere if we do not give it to them. This holds true on the opposite end as well. Women who have lesbian relationships are usually seeking emotional support, because most men do not know how to be intimate.

I know that this may seem to many an uncomfortable topic to discuss, but I guarantee you, if it is not exposed, it will continue to spread and men's lives will be destroyed because of it. Do we want to brush this under the rug or do we want to expose satan's schemes and allow souls to be delivered? This may not apply to you, but again, when we go into rebellion against our husbands, satan is there and anything can happen when we let him in the door. *My God!*

We do not realize the extent of what our refusal to submit to our husbands can lead to. We are walking a fine line. We need to catch this revelation before it is too late. Again, our husbands have free will to do as they wish, but what is your role in the marriage not being what God intended for it to be? Search your hearts and see what needs to change in you, and let God deal with him. Are you a *"fit"* for your husband?

Spiritual Suicide: Victory or Defeat?

I was a poster-child for all of the *"Women of God"* who would tell their husbands that they needed to analyze their walk with God. Instead of staying in my lane, as my husband says, I would tell him that he needed to read more, pray more, and fellowship more, so that he could grow in his walk with God. What I failed to realize was that I was the one who needed to analyze *"MY"* walk with the Lord. We need to ask ourselves these questions: *Are we really as close to God as we say we are?* If we are talking to our husbands, His Sons, in a derogatory manner, as some of us have done, I have to say that we are not. Stop allowing the enemy to deceive you ladies. He twists everything around in our lives to trick us and destroy our families.

> *"Be sober, be vigilant; because the adversary the devil walks about like a roaring lion, seeking whom he may devour."(1 Peter 5:8)*

He wants to destroy our marriages, but he has an agenda far more complex than that. Satan has been busy since the fall of man at trying to diminish God's seed in this earth. His plan in the Garden was to separate Adam and Eve and stop the plan of God from coming to pass.

> *"Take wives and beget sons and daughters; and take wives for your sons, and give your daughters to husbands, so that they may bear sons and daughters-that you may be increased there, and not diminished."(Jeremiah 29:6)*

The enemy ladies, has deceived us. Our husband is not the enemy, but satan. His goal is to separate husband and wife, so that the bond of marriage is broken and destroyed, which ultimately leads to the seed being diminished in the earth. This is where homosexuality comes into play. Satan confuses us so much, making us believe that our needs are not getting met, that we lose sight of what God's plan was for us in the beginning, which was:

> *"to be fruitful and multiply, fill the earth and subdue it. (Genesis 1:28)*

Satan tries to deceive us into believing that we are born homosexual, which is a lie from the pit of hell! He wants to diminish God's seed in this earth through sin. He wants us to be swallowed up in our sin, or as he puts it, *"Our choice on how to live our life"*. He is cunning, manipulative, persuasive, and sometimes even believable, look back at Eve. Women, I beseech you to stop satan dead in his tracks. He is destroying our families by using us as a pawn in his schemes, unbeknownst to us. He plays on our weakest attributes to lure us into his web of deceit. He is good if we let him have his way, but he is not that good. Our Lord, our Savior Jesus Christ has already defeated him. *GLORY TO GOD!*

God purposed for our husbands to be the head of their households and we know from Psalm 133:1-3 that God commanded a blessing when the people dwelt together in unity. It flows from the head; your husband, down upon the beard; you, the wife, and then down to the skirts of the garments, which signifies your children. Satan has even twisted this scripture by convincing us that we are capable of taking the spiritual reigns from our husbands and that God will bless our family by this. He is a worthless LIAR! Trust me. I already tried this and it did not work. It made my marriage worse, but the Spirit of the Living God stepped in and broke me, delivered me, and changed me!

We allow the enemy to twist our lives around so much that we even begin to twist God's Word to suit our own personal agendas in our marriages.

> *"And the oracle of the LORD you shall mention no more. For every man's word will be his oracle, for you have perverted the words of the living God, the LORD of hosts, our God."(Jeremiah 23:36)*

Women, return to the true and living Word of God. Stand firm on it and do not sway to the left or the right. There is only one straight path to the truth and that is the Word of God. Regain the power on the inside of you through consistent meditation on the Word, fellowshipping with the Lord in prayer, worshipping Him in the beauty of His holiness, and seeking His face through fasting. Use what God has given you women of God; what He purposed inside of you, to first destroy the seeds that you have allowed into your marriage: *insecurity, doubt, worry, pride, manipulation, greed, envying others, control, obsession, and vanity*. I am sure that there are many others, but these are just a few.

Break the chains of bondage from your marriages. Make a real decision to take your marriage back from the enemy. This will not happen by skimming through the Word, saying a quick "bless me" prayer, and then turning on your favorite soap opera and expecting God to do it for you. We should not be looking for a quick fix from God to restore a marriage that we messed up. He did not look for a quick fix when He was deciding a way for your salvation. *GLORY TO GOD!* He provided the ultimate sacrifice, His Son. So, we should expect to go through some things, in order to receive a breakthrough in our marriage.

> *"I protest by your rejoicing which I have in Jesus Christ, I die daily."(1 Corinthians 15:31, KJV)*

Paul is saying here that we will go through some things not only in our daily walk with God, but in our marriages. We have to deny ourselves and allow the Spirit of God to change us into what He wants us to be. We need to lie before the Lord and ask Him to cleanse us from all the evil that we have allowed to dwell in us.

We can take on many different spirits by not submitting. We have to cover ourselves in prayer and by reading His Word. Fasting is a good way to cleanse our spirits from evil.

> *"Is this not the fast that I have chosen: to loose the bonds of wickedness, to undo the heavy burdens, to let the oppressed go free, And that you break every yoke?"(Isaiah 58:6)*

Make a choice; decide today whether you want *VICTORY* or *DEFEAT*?

The Spirits

I want to discuss the many different kinds of spirits that become a part of us when we refuse to submit to our husbands. It is a progressive road to destruction and we will go over some of them, so that you can recognize them when they show their ugly faces.

As we begin to believe that there is something wrong with our husbands and we tell them that they need to change, these spirits automatically manifest themselves in us. We allow the enemy right in the door when we do not see immediate results from our husbands. We usually start out with *frustration*, because we do not see these results fast enough. We automatically assume that because we have confronted them with their *"so-called"* inadequacies that they are going to get a *"light bulb"* revelation and change. I do not want to burst your bubbles ladies, but this is not going to happen. You are frustrated, because it is not your job to change him. After so many instances of failed attempts to change our husbands, you would think that we would see the light and know that only God can change him, but we do not!

We continue to become even more frustrated and this frustration leads to *anger*. We get so mad, because we think that they are just not getting it. Now, instead of talking peacefully and rationally, our voices become louder and we begin to tell them what they *"Need"* to do, instead of encouraging them.

> *"It is better to dwell in a corner of the housetop, than with a brawling woman in a wide house." (Proverbs 21:9, KJV)*

If you had any hope of your husband changing, you have just destroyed it by your lack of self-control. No man wants to hear his wife nagging in his ear twenty-four hours a day. Most men know that they need to change and some actually desire to, but we make things worse, because of our lack of wisdom.

After anger takes root in our hearts, we eventually begin to start *resenting* our husbands, because we feel as if they are intentionally not growing or maturing as we feel they should. Have you ever felt like your husband does things, or does not do things, just to spite you? I have been there and it is a frustrating place to be in. You now find yourself in a position where you feel as if you are the one holding the family together, because he will not. Now you have invited not only frustration, anger, and resentment into the marriage, but now *bitterness*.

You begin to say and do things by lashing out at him. You start calling him names that in the end, you usually regret. Sarcasm begins to be a very frequent way of communication for you. You think that it will hurt him, but it usually ends up backfiring on you. Every avenue that you pursue leads to more frustration and you just let your mind wander for ways to get through to him, or better yet, back at him. Oh, the enemy loves this, ladies! He has started us on the road to destruction and this is only the beginning.

I have to say that I believed in my heart that everything I was doing was to help my husband. I thought I was well intentioned and that I was truly hearing from God concerning my husband, but I was being deceived. More than anything that shocked me about myself was to find out that I had allowed pride to form in my heart. You could not tell me that I had pride in me, but I did and it took a *BOLD* woman of God to reveal it to me before I could see it for myself. This may sound familiar to some of you. Once pride takes root, we begin to remind our husbands that we are the one who is going to church.

We tell them that we are the one who prays with our children and that we know, or think we know, the Word in and out. We have joined every ministry in the church, aside from taking the pastor's job, and forgotten that our main ministry begins at home with our husband.

We are so focused on his *"so-called"* shortcomings that we are losing ourselves in the process. Pride, if not dealt with quickly, can spread like cancer into all areas of your life.

"Pride goes before destruction and a haughty spirit before a fall."(Proverbs 16:18)

Issues of control begin to form where the spirit of pride is in operation. We begin to force ownership of certain areas that we feel he will not stand up and take charge of over his family. This is the point where you have taken the skirt off and stepped into the pants.

Oh, there is no turning back now, according to satan. You have assumed your husband's position; stepped into his role and now you are walking in his shoes. You have taken control. You have assumed the disciplinary role over your children, because you feel that he is immature and that he will not guide them correctly. You have told him that he is a worthless husband, but now you are telling him that he is a worthless father. Oh, this is good ladies, receive it!

You have taken over as the spiritual leader of your family, the disciplinary of the children and now you want to take over the finances, because you feel that you can do it better, the *"Eve Mentality"*. What is wrong with us ladies? How can we be so naïve to these spirits? We can, because we are sporting our *"spiritual halos"*. We feel that we are equipped by God to *"prophesy"* to our husbands and to tell them what the *"Spirit"* is saying. Wake up women! Stop trying to be so spiritual! God is not by any means impressed. We try to get so deep sometimes and do not even realize that we are the ones who are missing it. We truly act like we know it all and that we are the only one who is hearing from God.

"or did the word of God come originally from you? Or was it you only that it reached? (1 Corinthians 14:36)

We have to humble ourselves and realize that our husbands hear from God too, even if they do not share it with you. They probably do not share it with you, because you will criticize anything that they say and put them down. We are sinking deeper and deeper into the enemy's trap and we do not even know it. We have allowed our emotions to take us so far away from the truth that we begin to believe that our marriage has no hope. We feel as if our husband has pulled away from us, but most likely, you have pushed him away, because you do not know when to stop. We have entered into dangerous territory, because we have assumed a position only fit for God.

Another way that the enemy deceives us is by making us believe that we are doing these things for God and that He is directing us.

"For Satan himself transforms himself into an angel of light." (2 Corinthians 11:14)

This is not of God, but a trick from the enemy to pull us further away from God, as well as our husbands.

"Reality"

Once that we feel we have control over the spiritual care of our families, or more like taken control, nothing our husbands do seems to be enough for us. Everything our husbands do or say we put down and criticize, because it has not met our expectations or timetables. We are now acting as if we are God, but even our Father does not treat us like we treat our husbands. We have truly crossed the line! By this time, our husbands have reached their threshold with us. Now the spirits have transferred to him in the form of: *anger, rage, frustration, feelings of inadequacy, doubting himself as a man, a husband, and a father; depression, loneliness,* and many others that cause him to make decisions that he really does not want to make.

It is hard enough for our husbands to wake up every morning and know that they are held accountable for their families, without us provoking them on a daily basis.

> *"For what I am doing, I do not understand. For what I will to do, that I do not practice, but what I hate, that I do."*
> *(Romans 7:15)*

We have to realize that our husbands already face a multitude of temptations and war daily to make the right decisions. We can truly push a man to his limit, especially if he is not grounded in the Lord.

> *"A foolish son is the ruin of his father, and the contentions of a wife are a continual dripping." (Proverbs 19:13)*

Listen to this woman of God! We sound like a continual dripping to our husbands. Imagine the sound of water continually dripping from a faucet. It is irritating and aggravating. It continues, until we snap and run to turn it off, but it will not stop.

Sisters, hear what the Spirit is saying to you. When God is speaking to our husbands, they probably cannot hear Him clearly, because we are constantly in their ear. Our husbands can and do hear from God. It might not be what we think it should be, but they do hear. They may not act like it or act upon it right away, but this is not for you to know. Please remember that it is not your timing, but God's. We can push so hard sometimes to make something happen that is not ready to happen and we abort the plan that God has purposed for our husbands, or at least set it back many years.

God is not the author of confusion, but of peace. He is a God of order. He does not cause man, whom He created good, to fall under his wife. God created this order to keep peace within the boundaries of marriage. We want so much to live happy, peaceful, loving lives with our husbands. We want them to love us, cherish us, compliment us, and desire us. We want them to be our best friends and to trust us with their most intimate secrets inside of them. We want them to share their dreams and goals with us, but what are we doing to set the *atmosphere* for these things to take place?

For once, take your eyes and your mouth off of him and focus on you! What are you doing to make your husband feel safe and secure in your marriage? Are you encouraging him, not teaching or preaching, but lifting him up? No man wants a woman who does not appreciate him, who thinks she has to tell him who he is and what is best for him. Is this lifting up or tearing down? I understand that you really believe that you are helping him, so did I, but you are not! We are telling God that He is not doing His job and not doing it fast enough for us. Catch this ladies! How can we stand before God, worship Him, exalt Him above everything and everyone, and then turn around and betray Him by assuming that He is not well able to guide our husbands, His Sons.

What does this say about your walk with God? You are portraying yourself as a woman of God, but your actions are not in agreement with your words. Is this helping or hindering your husband? You are starting to look like a wolf in sheep's clothing. How do you expect him to be the man that God has called him to be when you are not being the woman that God has told you to be? We have to be grounded in the Word of God, having a firm foundation, to know that what we are hearing is from God and not the deceiver; satan.

> *"And when he brings out his own sheep, he goes before them, and the sheep follow him, for they know his voice. (Verse 5) "Yet they will by no means follow a stranger, but will flee from him, for they do not know the voice of strangers."(John 10:4-5)*

We have to allow God to go before us and lead us into His truth. This truth will reveal to you that when you leave from under His covering to marry, you now fall under the covering of your husband, your man of God; His Son.

> *"And Adam said: 'This is now bone of my bones and flesh of my flesh; she shall be called Woman, because she was taken out of man."(Genesis 2:23)*

Our husbands are a gift from the Lord. We would not be here if it were not for God pulling us out of man. We need to see how the Bible teaches women to carry themselves.

> *"Who can find a virtuous wife? For her worth is far above rubies, the heart of her husband safely trusts her; so he will have no lack of gain."(Proverbs 31:10)*

There is honor in this position, ladies. Satan wants us to believe that we need to be out in the spotlight, making decisions for our families, but this is not the heart of God for us. Verses 25-27 exemplify to me how a godly woman is to be.

> *"Strength and honor are her clothing; she shall rejoice in time to come." (Verse 26) "She opens her mouth with wisdom, and on her tongue is the law of kindness."(Verse 27) "She watches over the ways of her household, and does not eat the bread of idleness."(Proverbs 31:25-27)*

The key part in this scripture is she shall rejoice in *"time"* to come. As long as you are doing your job and doing it unto the Lord, He will acknowledge your service and reward you with a wonderful marriage.

Many of us do not understand this concept of service. If we all set aside our selfishness and understood that our first goal is to please the Lord, we would not have as many conflicts in our marriages as we do. Women do have a lot to do in the marriage. We go through nine months of pregnancy, hours (sometimes days) of labor, years of changing diapers and tedious chores such as cooking, cleaning, washing dishes and clothes, folding them, putting them away, and many other tasks throughout our days. This can become a burden to us if we are forgetting that our service is to the Lord.

If you think that you are doing this to please your children or your spouse, you will be living a long and unhappy life, because much of the work you do will never be acknowledged by your family. You have to see your role as a woman, a wife, and a mother, as service to God. You have to understand why you were created and get away from how society now portrays your role to be. Once you obtain peace about your existence, your life will never be the same again. Once you have confidence in yourself as a woman of God, satan cannot discourage or trick you. Once you have received revelation in your role as a wife, you will find it easier to submit to your husband and actually enjoy it! *HALLELUJAH!*

Required reading for the "serious" woman of God☺ Song of Solomon (The Shulamites's Words)

<u>Prayer for the Woman</u>

Father, I ask that You grant peace and purpose to every woman reading this book. I thank You in advance that lives have been touched and even changed as I speak this prayer. I thank You that as women, we now see how you purposed our lives to be; that we do hold a major role in our marriage, even though we are placed under the covering of our man of God. I pray that every woman has confidence and boldness in her "position", where other women will see them and ask, *"How do you do it?"* Humble us Father as we submit to the leading of our men of God, Your Sons. In Jesus' name. Amen.

Chapter 5
Submission in Marriage: "The Role of the Man"

It Takes Two to Tango

I know that if you are a man and you are reading this book, you are probably jumping up and down on the couch shouting, *"Thank God, someone finally gets it!"*, especially a woman? I know that you are ready as soon as you finish this book, and I pray that you do, to go and show this book to your wife or someone you know that you feel needs to submit, but hold that thought!

As in any relationship, man and woman, parent and child, or in any friendship, it takes two people to make the relationship work properly. Many people view submission as a problem that only women have. We have had this mentality etched into our minds by society since the beginning of time, but men can and do also possess the *"Eve Mentality"*. "What, you do have to be joking right?" Men cannot possess an "Eve Mentality", because Eve was a woman, not a man. Well I will definitely agree that Eve was not a man, but men can and do possess this kind of spirit.

Again, just to refresh your memory, this mentality is one where we isolate ourselves by believing that we do not need anyone to help us do anything. It is the *"I"* syndrome that we exposed in the last chapter. *"I"* want to do it my way; *"I"* am the husband, the head, and the *"MAN"*! Does this sound familiar to you? Well if it does not, I pray that after reading this book, you will make it a point to stay away from this type of mentality.

We saw from Genesis Chapter 3 that the serpent deceived Eve by isolating her from Adam, as well as God. The serpent entered in the door by asking a question, which Eve fell prey to. The Word shows us that Eve saw that the tree was good and it says,

> *"she also gave to her husband and he ate." (Genesis 3:6)*

So here, we see that it took two, Adam and Eve, to make a decision that God forbade them to make. It was not just Eve that sinned, but Adam as well.

> *"For Adam was not deceived, but the woman being deceived was in the transgression." (1Timothy 2:14)*

Even though Adam was not deceived, he did disobey God by receiving the fruit from his wife and because of this, he also received judgment from God.

> *"Then to Adam He said, 'Because you have heeded the voice of your wife, and have eaten from the tree of which I commanded you saying, "You shall not eat of it", "Cursed is the ground for your sake; in toil you shall eat of it all the days of your life." (Verse 18) "Both thorns and thistles it shall bring forth for you and you shall eat the herb of the field." (Verse 19) "In the sweat of your face, you shall eat bread till you re-*

turn to the ground, for out if it you were taken; For dust you are, and to dust you shall return."(Genesis 3:17-19)

The key to Adam receiving judgment was that he *heeded* the voice of his wife. This word in the King James Version is hearkened, which is derived from the Hebrew word *shama*, which means *to hear intelligently, give attention, or obedience.* Could you imagine how God felt when Adam hearkened to the voice of Eve, and not of Him? Adam obeyed Eve's insisting and disobeyed His Creator. He heeded to the one who was taken *"out"* of him. This is not order.

This is how our marriages are functioning today. Men are not fulfilling their roles as head of the family.

"For the husband is the head of the wife, as also Christ is head of the church; and He is the Savior of the body." (Ephesians 5:23)

Men need to stand up and walk in this God ordained authority. You should not be allowing your wives to run your household. Many of you have refused to be the head, so your wives have had to assume a role that they are not equipped to handle and do not want, in the beginning. She begins to take on, not only her role, but yours as well, and you are just sitting back and relaxing, while satan is having a field day in your home.

Men, this is not cute. You are bragging to your friends that your wife *"does it all"* and actually fall into the trap of thinking, *"you are the man"*. Oh, you are the man; a foolish man! The devil loves the fact that you do not have a clue. He not only tries to twist the woman's role, but he twists yours too. Men need to accept this role as head, not only for their benefit, but also for the benefit of their wives and children. God has created in you something that only you can carry out as a man. There is potential down on the inside of you that is fighting to come to the surface. Stop being passive in your role as husband and assert yourself, not forcefully, but with the knowledge of who God created you to be.

Standing on the Word

The enemy attacks men more than women in the area of studying the Word of God. Men were raised to go to work at a very young age and were not encouraged to read or write, as women were. They were told that they were the providers and if they did not work, they did not eat. The Bible also says this, but the enemy twists it so that we miss what the real revelation of it is. Men are still doing this today. They take their jobs, or whatever the distraction may be, as an excuse as to why they cannot study the Word of God.

This is what satan wants for you men. He knows that when you make a commitment to God's Word, he is done! When women make this commitment, satan is not moved, because he knows he can easily tempt them with manipulation, because their husband may not be stepping up. When men catch the vision of headship, heaven opens up over their lives; godly order is activated, and everyone assumes their roles in which they were created. *HALLELUJAH!*

Satan already planned ahead of time that he would tempt Eve and not Adam; because he knew he would not deceive Adam. Adam knew his role as a subduer and one who had dominion, but where he failed was in his role as head. He allowed his emotions to cloud his judgment as well. Men can do this too, not just women! Adam handed his authority over to Eve without even a thought that he may be disobeying God's command. Men need to learn from Adam's mistake and grow from it. You are handing the authority that God gave you over to your wives with not even a thought that she may be taking you straight to hell. Hear what the Spirit is saying men. You are held accountable for your family, not your wife. If you allow her to assume this role and she messes it up, you will have to answer for it, not her.

God made you the head of your wife and He did this because He knows how He created man and woman to be; how they would fit together in the roles that He designed them for. Marriage is like a puzzle, if one piece is missing or if one is in the wrong position, the puzzle cannot be made, it has no purpose and is useless. This is what the enemy wants for us. He confuses our roles to such an extent that we just give up and throw away our marriages.

Rise up my brothers! Stand against satan and put him under your feet! Do not be held accountable for the demise of your marriage. Get into the Word of God and find out how to be a husband. Stop making excuses like, *"She will not get off of my back"*, *"My boss is working me like a slave"*, *"and I am just not a reader like she is"*, and all the other ones you use to excuse yourself from reading God's Word. It is simple, you want to be blessed or you do not. Either you will submit to God, or you will not. God will not force you to make a decision either way. He created you with a free will to choose. Now if you choose to submit to Him and allow Him to bless you, then you have some work to do.

When you desire a promotion at work, you do your best work to obtain it, right? When someone takes something that is rightfully yours, you do everything possible to get it back, right? This is how God desires for you to get what He has for you.

"Then Jacob was left alone; and a Man wrestled with him until the breaking of day. Now when He saw that He did not prevail against him, He touched the socket of his hip; and the socket of Jacob's hip was out of joint as He wrestled him. And He said, 'Let Me go, for the day breaks. But he said, "I will not let you go until you bless me!" (Genesis 32:24-26)

GLORY TO GOD! Jacob *REFUSED* to let go of God, until He blessed him. Even when Jacob's hip was out of joint, he pressed on to receive his blessing. God told Jacob to let him go, but Jacob said *NO!* Now Jacob was considered a "heel-catcher", which meant that he was always fighting to get his way out of something, but mostly being a deceiver. He began by deceiving his brother Esau out of his birthright, whom he wrestled with in his mother's womb by actually grabbing the heel of his brother Esau. Twenty years after leaving his home and knowing that Esau was angry with him for stealing his birthright and his father's blessing, he met a *"Man"* and wrestled all night with Him. Jacob was used to fighting his way out of things, so he continued to fight this time, until he was blessed.

Can we come to God in this manner? Does it not sound like we are telling God what to do? If scripture references this event, then God is trying to show us something through it. God desires for all men to seek after Him with their whole hearts and receive *ALL* that He has laid up for them. This scripture leads us to believe that Jacob was tired of doing things his own way and desired a change. God saw this and chose to *"touch him"* in such a way that would humble Jacob and show him that he could indeed change his ways.

In verse 27 it says, *"So He said to him, 'What is your name?'" "He said, 'Jacob'." (Verse 28) "And He said, 'Your name shall no longer be called Jacob, but Israel, for you have struggled with God and with men, and have prevailed."*

Jacob's character had indeed changed. Jacob, once the ambitious deceiver, has now become Israel, the one who struggles with God and overcomes. Pressing his way to receive his blessing, God changed his name to Israel and because of that pressing, his persistence, and his commitment to get *ALL* that God had for him, God blessed him right there.

Israel is derived from the Hebrew word *Yisrael*, which means *he will rule as God*. Jacob is derived from the Hebrew word *Yaaqob*, which means *heel-catcher*. God said in Genesis 32 that Jacob wrestled with Him, as well as man, so this is why he was referenced as a heel-catcher. Jacob refused to give in to anyone, including God and because of that, he was given a name of influence, a name of authority. God said Jacob would now be called Israel, one who rules as God!

Men of God, this should be the means by which you receive God's blessings. Go after God as Jacob did and *REFUSE* to leave Him alone, until He blesses you. Many would say this is disrespectful to God, but God Himself was pleased with Jacob's refusal to leave

Him alone. It moved God to see such passion and boldness in this man to change his lifestyle and to get what he desired from the Lord.

What have you done lately that has *moved* God to want to bless you? God honored Jacob by giving him a new name. What name will God change yours too? What name will He etch in the Spirit on your behalf? What name will follow you and your family throughout this earth?

When your wife sees the authority that you have committed to walk in operating in your life, she will not know how to react at first. Order is shifting on your behalf in heaven and satan is becoming nervous. He will go on the offensive with your wife by telling her that you are trying to control her, but this should be the time where you throw yourself into the Word of God even more. Find out how God desires you to use your authority given to you in marriage. Do not allow satan to distort this authority and cause you to misuse it and threaten your marriage.

Seek the wisdom of God for your marriage and for your role in that marriage. Do not allow the enemy to gain any ground in your life by refusing to receive knowledge and understanding from the very One who created marriage, God the Father.

"Get wisdom! Get understanding! Do not forget, nor turn away from the words of my mouth." (Proverbs 4:5)

God has a word for every situation that we will ever go through in this life. We just have to seek His Word and find it. It takes work and the question is, *"How bad do you want your marriage to work?"* What are you willing to go through to receive the blessings of God?

Your Queen "Esther"

The first step, after finding out what your role is, I believe, is to get to know how God sees your wife, His daughter. God desires for you a wonderful marriage; a marriage of joy, peace, and love; a marriage that is set apart for His glory.

"Husbands love your wives just as Christ also loved the church and gave Himself for her." (Verse 26) "that He might sanctify and cleanse her with the washing of water by the Word." (Verse 27) "that He might present her to Himself a glorious church, not having spot or wrinkle or any such thing, but that she should be holy and without blemish."(Ephesians 5:25-27)

Husbands, look at the responsibility that God has given you! God gave you the power, through love, to cover your wives and cause her to be holy, without blemish. *WOW!* That is an awesome gift. I have heard many husbands criticize their believing wives for being *"holier than thou"*, if you will.

Men, this is how you should desire your wife to be; a woman who carries your name with integrity, loyalty, and yes, even authority; a woman who is known in the community as a true woman of God; a kind, compassionate, loving, patient, gentle, faithful, and yes, *holy* woman of God.

Do not allow satan to confuse you into believing that your wife is above you, because she is grounded in the Word. Again, if you understand your purpose as a man of God and walk in the authority that He has given you, her character will compliment your role as a husband and cause your marriage to blossom. This is how God intended for Adam and Eve to walk in marriage. When we walk in our designed purposes, as God created us to be, order is established and life becomes much easier.

Begin to see your wife as God sees her. The woman that you envisioned your wife to be is the one that you have, you just have to pray for her and cover her, so that she may blossom into that woman of God. Esther was a woman whom people respected. She had such an air about her that made people draw to her.

> *"So it was, when the king saw Queen Esther standing in the court, that she found favor in his sight, and the king held out to Esther the golden scepter that was in his hand. Then Esther went near and touched the top of the scepter."(Esther 5:2)*

Esther found favor in the sight of the king, because of her character. Your wife should be that woman to you. She should have such favor in your sight that whatever she desires should be granted unto her, because of her integrity and faithfulness. Most men cannot look at their wives in this manner, because of the way society looks at the woman today. Men see women as *"gold diggers"* and this is why they do not shower their wives with love, kindness, compassion, and yes, even gifts. Men go into marriage with the *WRONG* ideals of how they should treat their wives. Marriage is a two-way street, not a one-way street. When the both of you are fulfilling your roles in the relationship, you will set out to please one another and live a wonderful life together.

Make your wife feel like she is the *"Esther"* in your life. Let her know that she is a woman of influence who represents her husband well. You have to speak those things into her life to encourage her that she is a wonderful woman of God and that you are honored to have her in your life. If you desire the fulfilled marriage that I know we all want, erase whatever thoughts the *"world"* has given you about women and find out who God says they are.

You are not of this World

We make life difficult for ourselves, because either we blame our spouse for the marriage not working or we refuse, through pride, to be what God wants us to be. Many men try to live up to the standard of what the "world" wants them to be.

> *"They are not of this world, just as I am not of the world." (John 17:16)*

God desires to separate us from the world and submit to His order in marriage, because He created it. Again, I will say only the creator of something or someone knows its purpose. So trust in Him and find out what His Word says about it and do it.

> *"Husbands, love your wives and do not be bitter toward them". (Colossians 3:19)*

Many times husbands become bitter towards their wives because of decisions that she has made for their family. You have to understand that you are the one who allowed her to make those decisions by not stepping up and being the head of your home. You are not bitter with her, but yourself, because you *KNOW* that you did not take the responsible path as a husband. God says not to be bitter towards your wife, His daughter.

> *"So husbands ought to love their own wives as their own bodies; he who loves his wife loves himself. For no one ever hated his own flesh, but nourishes and cherishes it, just as the Lord does the church." (Ephesians 5:28-29)*

Love is a choice. If you do not know the love of God, you will suffer in this world, but God made this command easier as it pertains to marriage. If you love yourself, you love your wife, because you are one flesh. She is now a part of you. Love her and cherish her just as Christ does the church, and gave His life for her. To know how to love as Christ does, you have to read the Word. Only those who are willing to love their wives as Christ loved the church will prosper.

I hear so many men, Christians as well, complaining because their marriages are a mess, their job is stressful, their children are disobedient, their finances are looking funny, and the world is on their shoulders. Do you want to spend the rest of your life complaining or are you willing to do something about it?

> *"If you are willing and obedient, you shall eat the good of the land; but if you refuse and rebel, you shall be devoured by the sword. For the mouth of the Lord has spoken."(Isaiah 1:19-20)*

God is giving you a way of escape men. He does not want you to suffer, but wants you to succeed and prosper. His way is always best even if it does not feel good at the time.

> *"There is a way that seems right to a man, but its end is the way of death."(Proverbs 14:12)*

Choose the way of the Lord for your marriage and allow the Spirit of the Lord to guide you in the order that He would have you to be in as a husband to His daughter. Allow yourself the opportunity to change as Jacob did and watch God bless you like never before.

Many men fail to recognize the importance of being a godly man, because of the breakdown of the moral fabric of our society. Two of the biggest causes of this are sex and money. The media, from television, magazines, billboards, and the internet, sensationalizes sex and gives men no sense of responsibility when it comes to women. Men either bring these spirits into the marriage or pick them up afterwards and begin to treat their wives as they view these other women. This is not of God and only leads to loneliness men. The enemy tries to capture men with visual stimulation and fleshly desires, but this is addiction, which means that you will have to continue to feed these things into your flesh to fulfill your needs. This is no way to live.

> *"For all that is in this world--the lust of the flesh, the lust of the eyes and the pride of life--is not of the Father but is of the world."(1 John 2:16)*

This scripture also holds true for the love of money. Again, we see entertainers who are *"living it up"*, as they view it. They throw money around on ridiculous things and boast about their lifestyles, when in reality, they are miserable! The media shows these people on a daily basis living the lifestyle of the rich and famous, while they are on their fourth, fifth, and even sixth marriage. Money does not guarantee happiness men, only God does. *HALLELUJAH!*

"But those who desire to be rich fall into temptation and a snare, and into many foolish and harmful lusts, which drown men in destruction and perdition."(Verse 10) "For the love of money is the root of all kinds of evil, for which some have strayed from the faith in their greediness, and pierced themselves through with many sorrows."(1Timothy 6:9-10)

Of these, neither the lust of sex, nor the love of money will bring you happiness or prosperity. Stop allowing the devil to deceive you brothers. He is a LIAR from the pit of hell! The best way for a man to denounce these spirits is to connect to a true Word teaching, Holy Spirit filled church; a place where he will not be judged by how he feels, but encouraged by other brothers who have been through, or are going through the same things themselves. Men need to see examples of godly men who are living right and truly receiving the blessings of God in their lives because of it; men whose marriages are displaying the love of God and whose wives submit to them freely, because they have assumed their roles as head of their families.

These relationships are vital for a man and the enemy tries his best to keep you away from them.

"As iron sharpens iron, so a man sharpens the countenance of his friend."(Proverbs 27:17)

Desire these friendships; pursue them with all diligence, so that you may build one another up in the Lord. This also gives you a means of accountability. You will have someone in whom you can confide in when things get tough in your marriage. As you begin to walk in confidence as a man of God, submission becomes an easier word to swallow. It is a process men, and listen to *NO* one who tells you that it is easy for them, because submission comes from denying your flesh and its desires and this is easy for no one! It takes commitment, dedication, and a willingness to obey God no matter what the cost.

Once you have submitted to the accountability of your brothers, you will find that you will be able to submit to your pastor, the man or woman that God has placed over your life to pour into your life. After you have committed to consistent fellowship with your brothers and a local body, your views on being a man of God will change. It cannot help but change if you are planted in a Word teaching, Holy Spirit filled church. The examples of your man and woman of God will teach you how to have a godly marriage and those under them should be walking in this same manifestation.

Allow others to strengthen you in your walk with the Lord. We need one another in order to accomplish this. Remember, men can also possess the *"Eve Mentality"*. When you say, *"I do not need anyone to tell me how to live my life"*, you are walking in that spirit. God did not intend for us to go through this life alone and depressed. The enemy wants us to isolate ourselves from others, so that we cannot be encouraged and strengthened. He wants us to believe that we are the only ones going through this battle, and that if we tell someone, they will judge us. Do not believe these lies men. God gave us one another to edify and comfort each other in this walk. He wants us to depend on one another and hold each other up when we fall.

> *"Confess your trespasses to one another, and pray for one another, that you may be healed. The effective fervent prayer of a righteous man avails much." (James 5:16)*

We have to know what His Word says, so that satan's devices do not trick us. We do not know what to do, because we do not read and meditate on our guide in this life, the Word of God.

"lest Satan should take advantage of us; for we are not ignorant of his devices." (2 Corinthians 2:11)

We are only ignorant if we do not read His Word. Meditate on it and find out not only who God is, but how satan works, so you can be prepared when he comes.

Judas encountered isolation when he plotted with the priests and the elders to hand Jesus over to be put to death. Judas was given not only the other disciples to encourage him, but he had Jesus right there with him. God gave Judas people in whom he could go and confess his trespasses to, so that they could pray for him that he may be forgiven, but he chose to isolate himself.

"Then he threw down the pieces of silver in the temple and departed, and went and hanged himself." (Matthew 27:5)

This is what satan wants us to do. He deceives us into believing that no one understands us and leads us into a dark hole that we cannot come out of, like Judas.

The devil is a LIAR! *DO NOT* let him take your life from you. Stand up and become *EMPOWERED* through the Word of God, so that you can know your enemy, and that enemy is not your wife! Satan loves to twist the truth and blind us, so that we are unable to tell the difference. He tries to place enmity between husband and wife to such an extent that we say we wish that we had never met them. This is absolutely ridiculous! This can only be the workings of the devil. You have to see this for what it is. Stop allowing the enemy to have his way in your marriage.

Confess and Believe

All right, I believe that you now understand why you have been unable to see results in your marriage. You have been equipped with the tools available to be able to recognize satan when he comes to separate you from your spouse. Now, you need to recognize your wife as the woman God created her to be for you and continue confessing these things into her life.

The biggest problem that we have in this world is what we confess into our own lives. Men, speak to your wives as God speaks to her. The love that God has for us all is the kind of love that He would give for His only Son. This is love! God is love and He commands you to love your wife even as Christ loved the church and gave His life for her. Begin to renew your mind, look to the scriptures to see what a godly woman looks like and begin to confess it over your wife.

> *"He who finds a wife finds a good thing and obtains favor from the Lord."(Proverbs 18:22)*

The enemy wants you to believe that she is a curse, but God says she is a good thing and you find favor with the Lord because she is your wife. *Hallelujah!*

You receive benefits from the Lord on her behalf. Most men confess with their mouths, *"if you were not married to me, you would have nothing"*. Re-think what you are saying men, God says something different.

> *Your wife shall be like a fruitful vine in the very heart of your house, your children like olive plants all around your table."(Psalm 128:3)*

Your wife is a blessing from God, sent to fill a space inside of you that needs her and she causes your home to be filled with joy, if you allow her to.

Just as I said in the last chapter to the women, *"Stop causing your husbands to doubt their manhood"*, I tell you, *"Stop causing your wives to doubt who they are as women"*. Women are sensitive and emotional beings. They need to be nurtured, caressed, and cared for with gentleness and kindness. This is how a woman responds to her husband. If you want your wives to blossom and spring forth into that Proverbs 31 *"Virtuous Woman"*, which she is already, build her up and encourage her in the role that God created for her and let her know that you are grabbing the reins back and assuming your God-given role as the head of your family.

Brothers, women want you to step up into this position, not pridefully, but humbly. It is yours, so you do not have to justify it, just walk in it! *GLORY TO GOD!* If you want your wives to submit to you and reverence you, then you need to get back at the helm of the ship and steer her, guide her, and dock her as God leads you in love! She is your responsibility. Her nurturing, her guidance, her self-esteem, and even her spiritual leading should be led by her covering; her head; her husband. The respect you desire will only come when she sees how much you love and care for her. There is order in the spiritual, as well as the natural.

> *"However, the spiritual is not first, but the natural, and afterward the spiritual."(1 Corinthians 15:46)*

God is telling us that because we are man, we need natural love first, physical and emotional, before he will bless us spiritually, where we can begin to prosper in this life.

We have to understand that faith is saying something and doing something. Again, what you confess with your mouth over your wife and begin to show her by your actions that you believe it, is faith. Faith believes that it is even if you do not see it right away. Faith is work brothers. Marriage takes a lot of work and I believe that you only need three things to achieve a loving marriage: *Unity, Determination, and a Willingness to want MORE!* You both have to fight for what you want and put the enemy under your feet!

I will close with these last scriptures, because they continue to ring in my spirit.

> *"Live joyfully with your wife whom you love all the days of your vain life, which He has given you under the sun, all your days of vanity; for that is your portion in life, and in the labor which you perform under the sun." (Verse 10) "Whatever your hands find to do, do it with your might; for there is no work or device or knowledge or wisdom in the grave where you are going."(Ecclesiastes 9:9-10)*

WOW! It is that simple! Selah. *GLORY TO HIS NAME!*

Required reading for the "serious" man of God☺ Song of Solomon (The Beloved's Words)

Prayer for the Man

I pray Lord that every man that reads the words of these pages will have a new perspective on how to live as a true man of God. I pray that their eyes have been opened to the devices of satan, so that they will no longer be held captive by his lies. I pray that they have allowed Your Word to transform their lives and Your Holy Spirit to guide them. I declare *Victory* in their lives and in their marriages. I stand in agreement with Your Word in 1 John 5:14-15, which says,

> *"Now this is the confidence that we have in Him, that if we ask anything according to His Will, He hears us. And if we know He hears us, whatever we ask, we know that we have the petitions that we have asked of Him."*

Selah!

Chapter 6
Submission: Holding One Another Accountable

The Order of Accountability

We can submit in many different ways, not just in marriage. In a world that is full of chaos, we need some sense of order and accountability to live a peaceable life. The word order is defined as *the prescribed form or customary procedure*. This word is derived from the Hebrew word *arak*, which means *to set in a row, arrange, to put (set) in array, compare, direct, equal, esteem, estimate, expert, furnish, or handle*. Without order in our lives, we tend to accept anything that comes our way. There is no system of balance and we begin to lose sight of who we are and what our real purpose in life is. There are too many *"things"* distracting us. We allow things, as well as other people, to decide who and what we are. This is a very dangerous way to live your life.

Just as there is a purpose for order in our marriage, there is a purpose for order in our everyday lives.

"The steps of a good man are ordered by the Lord and He delights in his way." (Psalm 37:23)

Our steps are ordered by God if we allow Him to order them. God does not force His Will upon our lives, but offers it freely to those who receive it willingly. When we refuse this order, we will have confusion in our lives. We saw from Genesis that Eve refused order established by God and disobeyed His command to not eat of the forbidden tree, and look at the result of her disobedience.

The word order has a definite relationship to the word submit. When there is established order to a thing, a person, or situation it is understood that submission is necessary to keep that order flowing. It is amazing how we allow our lives to get so out of order when God established a way of peace if we would only submit to it. A good way of keeping the order flowing in your life is to have someone who can hold you accountable to that order. The word accountable is defined as *liable to being called to account; answerable*. This word is derived from the Greek word *logos*, which means *something said; reasoning, motive, account, cause, communication, or intent*.

We should all have someone that we need to answer to or that can reason with us to keep us on track. I have a wonderful friend who has kept in contact with me from the day that I left for Germany three years ago. We stay in regular communication, whether by phone or e-mail, and hold one another accountable in our walk with God. There is *ALWAYS* a Word from the Lord to encourage and lift us up in our conversations. We understand that we need one another and accept correction or counsel when it is offered, because we trust the God in each other. Our relationship is mutual and there is a respect on both sides that never needs to be mentioned, it is just evident. We both have grown together in the Lord and matured together through our mistakes. As believers, we need someone to hold us up and to edify us.

The word edify is defined as *to instruct, especially so as to encourage intellectual, moral, or spiritual improvement; to build up, establish, or strengthen a person; to uplift.* This word is derived from the Greek word *oikodomeo*, which means *to be a house builder, construct, confirm, build (-er, -ing, up) edify, or embolden.* We have the power to be *"house builders"* people. As we encourage others, we build them up in the Lord, we edify them. They become emboldened because of our communication with them. They see your love and know that you care for them, which gives them a sense of belonging.

"Therefore comfort each other and edify one another, just as you also are doing." (1 Thessalonians 5:11)

They are more apt to receiving God's Word as truth, instead of just an old text that is outdated, when you are sharing yourself with them and building them up. What you are communicating to them in love is being confirmed as they fellowship with the Lord. There is power in holding one another accountable; it is establishing order in your lives.

As you purpose to be there to hold someone accountable, you too are being established to account for your walk. You too now have someone who can encourage you, strengthen you, uplift you, and build you up; to embolden you to face whatever mountain you may be facing. This is why God tells us to be in constant fellowship.

"And let us consider one another in order to stir up love and good works, not forsaking the assembling of ourselves together, as in the manner of some, but exhorting one another, and so much more as you see the Day approaching." (Hebrews 10:24-25)

God tells us to exhort one another. The word exhort is defined as *to urge by strong, often stirring argument, admonition, advice, or appeal; to urge on or encourage.* This word is derived from the Greek word *parakaleo*, which means *to call near, invite, invoke (by implora-*

tion, hortation, or consolation) beseech, call for (be of good) comfort, desire, (give) exhort, entreat, or pray.

We need one another to be real with each other. We do not need someone to tell us that we need help and to go find it somewhere else. We have to have someone who will urge us through advice, encouragement, and prayer.

We are believers, but we are not exempt from going through trials and tribulation in this life. How we handle our problems will reveal who we are in this world. This will not happen if you cannot accept that you are not in this life alone! *WE NEED ONE ANOTHER!* As you become accustomed to the advice of a fellow believer, you will know when someone comes along who is not serious about real fellowship. Never allow yourself to be caught up with someone who is always negative. It is said that you are or will become like the people who you hang around the most. When you are in need of exhortation, do not go and call the neighborhood *"busybody"*. As soon as you call, before you can even get your name out, they are spilling everyone's business out in the street.

Be mindful of the people in whom you place your trust and confidence. Do not allow the enemy place to make you think that you can share your time with just anyone and it not harm you spiritually. There are those who have no vision for their lives at all, so why would they uplift you in your vision. More often than not, they will try to dissuade you into believing that you can never achieve such a goal.

> *"Do not be unequally yoked together with unbelievers. For what fellowship has righteousness with lawlessness? And what communion has light with darkness?"(2 Corinthians 6:14)*

We have to fellowship with believers who are serious about their walk with God, those of *"like faith"*. Even if someone goes to church on a regular basis and attends every meeting and is at every function, does not mean that they can be trusted with your most intimate secrets. Guard yourselves and the anointing on your lives.

You would not go out and give the number of your bank account to a stranger would you? This is exactly what happens to us, as believers, when we share our visions and dreams with just anyone, they will *"Wipe us out!"* They will see what God is doing in your life and become jealous, because they have refused to seek God for the vision and purpose for their own lives. They will begin to discourage you and have you questioning what God has already told you.

Remove yourselves immediately from this type of fellowship if you are in it! Allowing yourself to spend time with these kinds of people will lead you to despair; it is not fruitful. Begin to get to know your brothers and sisters in Christ, so that you can be certain of who you can confide in. Use wisdom in seeking godly fellowship. As you do, you will begin to feel many burdens lifted from you. You will no longer feel as though you are the only one going through something.

When you find that someone in whom you can share your burdens with, they will pray for you and encourage you in the Word. They will also rejoice with you when God blesses you, and not become jealous and envious.

> *"Therefore let us pursue the things which make for peace and the things by which one may edify another."(Romans 14:19)*

Allow another believer to be that one who can share in your burdens and be there for you. The word burden is defined as *something carried; a responsibility or duty*. This word is derived from the Greek word *baros*, which means *weight, load, abundance, or authority*. We, as believers, are not immune from hurt, pain, or *"life"*. We have to carry some things. We have weights that we will hold in our walk with God. Jesus held the ultimate weight of our sins all the way to the cross. He carried our burdens to death. We have to go through to get to what God has for us, but He does not leave us alone to do this. We have others to hold us accountable and to bear our burdens with us. Galatians 6:2 says,

> *"Bear one another's burdens, and so fulfill the law of Christ."*

God knows that we cannot make it alone in this life. As the body of Christ, we are held accountable by God for what we do and do not do in His Son's name. We have received His infallible Word and it says to bear one another's burdens and so fulfill the law of Christ. We are taking on just a portion of what He took for us on Calvary. Do this with joy and thanksgiving to the Father and do not complain in it. Did Jesus complain when He took your sins at the cross? He gives us what we need; we just have to accept it and submit to it.

Do you now believe that you have a responsibility to your fellow believers? Do you now understand that you need one another to fulfill the law of Christ? Please do not go through this life alone thinking that you can survive on your own, because this is pride and I can guarantee you that God is not walking with you when you have pride in your heart, the *"Eve Mentality"*. Make a commitment today, if you have not already, to have someone hold you accountable in your walk with God. In return, give yourself wholly in support of another who needs to be held accountable. God needs us to be the "body" of Jesus in this earth. When you bear the burden of another soul in this earth, you are showing them Jesus. *GLORY TO GOD!*

Prayer for Accountability

Father, we thank You for the leading of the Holy Spirit. We submit ourselves to one another this day and thank You for godly relationships that will be formed in our lives. Move us away from believing that we can do it all on our own and show us that we need one another in the earth to fulfill Your purposes in our lives. In Jesus' name. Amen.

Chapter 7
Submission to Authority

Who's the BOSS?

      We have gone over submission in marriage and submission as it pertains to the accountability of believers. I believe that these types of submission can be easier accomplished, because of the love that we have for our spouses and the friendships that we have with our brothers and sisters. Now we will transition into an area where many people find it hard to submit; *AUTHORITY!* We can get passed the authority in marriage, because we understand that we all have different roles, or positions, that cause harmony within our marriages, but we also have to understand that the same holds true for our jobs and even our government.

      The word authority is defined as *the power to enforce laws, exact obedience, command, determine or judge; the power or right to give orders or make decisions.* This word is derived from the Greek word *exousia*, which means *privilege, force, capacity, competency, freedom, mastery, delegated influence, authority, jurisdiction, liberty, power, right, or strength.* It is very hard to submit to this type of authority. We all feel that we are our own person and that no one has a right to tell us what to do. We go and apply for a job and as soon as we get our foot in the door, we are trying to run things. We begin to feel like we can do a better job than the one who is there. *Slow down!* Analyze yourself and see why you are where you are. What is your motive for doing the things that you do? I can guarantee you that if you value the job that you have, you will submit to your employer, before you end up not having a job. That person was there before you and they will most likely be there when you are gone.

We have to understand that no matter what position we are in, we have to submit to someone's authority. In our everyday lives, we see people in positions of authority. Our local law enforcement personnel are here to enforce local laws from how fast we drive our cars to making sure that drugs stay off of our street corners. We, as citizens, have to submit to their authority or we can suffer the consequences. They are in authority to keep peace on our streets and to keep us safe.

They too, as local law enforcement, have to submit to a higher authority, which is the state. The state has a different set of laws to enforce, so they are governed by different standards. They may have more responsibilities than the local do, but they too are subject to a higher authority, the federal government. The federal government can many times take over jurisdiction, or authority, from either of these positions, because of their delegated influence.

We have to understand that God sets everything in order as it pleases Him, even our government. We may not see it because of all of the corruption involved in government, but it is still there, whether we like it or not.

"Therefore I exhort first of all that supplications, prayers, intercessions, and giving of thanks be made for all men, for kings and

all who are in authority, that we may lead a quiet and peaceable life in all godliness and reverence."(1Timothy 2:1-2)

No matter what we see on the news about politicians and those in authority, we are exhorted to pray for them and give thanks for them. The next verse says that this is good and acceptable to God. We have to stop listening to other people's opinions on authority figures.

We have many people of influence like actors, celebrities, and others who are bashing our president for his beliefs and for his decisions that he has made as president. Even if you do not agree with all of his decisions, you are still required by God to submit to his authority.

> *"Therefore submit yourselves to every ordinance of man for the Lord's sake, whether to the kings as supreme," (verse 14) "or to governors, as to those who are sent by him for the punishment of evildoers and for the praise of those who do good." Verse 15 says, "For this is the will of God……." (1 Peter 2:13-15)*

Our president, as well as every one before him, has had to deal with many complex decisions that need to be resolved. He does not just sit back and take these decisions lightly. He also has to submit to those in authority who may have more experience than he may in certain areas, to make a just decision. This calls for a great deal of humility. Just as we submit ourselves to God for godly marriages and godly friendships, we have to submit to God in order to understand why it is so important to submit to our leaders. God established leadership in the earth to bring about order and peace. Without designated authority over our lives, there would be chaos in our world. Everyone in authority has a higher authority in which they are subject to.

> *"All the leaders and the mighty men, and also all the sons of King David, submitted themselves to King Solomon."(1 Chronicles 29:24)*

Why do you believe that God talked so much about authority in the Bible? He knew that without it, we would be a rebellious people. If we cannot submit to authority in the earth, how can we submit to God, who created it? We have to begin to look at submission through the *"eyes"* of God, and this is His Word.

Now that we have a foundation of knowing that we are to submit to authority figures no matter what we feel or believe about them, we can move on to the influence of authority. Many people who hold authoritative positions become entangled in the status of such a position. They begin to accept ideals from others who are in their circle of influence just to fit in, causing them to take advantage of that position. We see this in our government through politicians. They are by no means the only ones, but it is more prevalent among this group of people. We have seen the embezzling of money, accepting of bribes, defrauding the government however they can, and many other unacceptable crimes. They feel that they are untouchable, because many of their peers are doing the same things. What they all lack is leadership themselves.

When these new politicians come in, they are *"mentored"* by those who have been in the game for a long time, *"corrupt politicians"*. They are drawn in by the lifestyles that they see; the money, the homes, the cars, and all of the other *"perks"* of being a politician, but this is only temporary; it will not last.

> *"For the leaders of this people cause them to err, and those who are led by them are destroyed."(Isaiah 9:16)*

If you are in a position of authority, it is your responsibility to lead the people under you with integrity. The only way for them to become good leaders is from their example. If you hold a position and have influence, you should be using that influence to build your peers up, not to tear them down by usurping that authority to meet your own personal needs.

> *"When the righteous are in authority, the people rejoice; but when the wicked man rules, the people groan."(Proverbs 29:2)*

Those of you in authority have more power than you realize; not the power that you have been using, but the power to build up nations of honorable men and women. Instead of using your authority to weaken, use it to strengthen. Instead of looking out for your own personal gain, make it your life's goal to look out for the growth and maturity of those under you. There is much more satisfaction in leaving a legacy of raising a generation of men and women of authority who hold integrity than *"gaining the whole world and losing your soul"*.

All throughout the Old Testament, we saw many different kings rise to power. The majority of them were destroyed, because of their refusal to submit to God. They were selfish and greedy men who kept those under them bound in slavery, as they grew wealthier by the hour. Others led their people under them with all diligence and compassion; who gave their entire lives in service to these people.

The word king is defined as *one that is supreme or preeminent in a particular group, category, or sphere*. This word is derived from the Hebrew word *malak*, which means *to reign, to ascend to the throne, to induct into royalty*. The word leader is defined as *a person who rules, guides, or inspires others*. This word is derived from the Hebrew word *nagid*, which means *a commander (civil, military or religious), honorable, captain, chief, excellent thing, governor, leader, noble prince, or ruler*.

The reason I was led to show these differences in definitions, as well as all of the others in this book, is to allow the reader to distinguish between how the world views these words and how God intended for them to have their purpose. A king's desire is to reign and rule. He does not concern himself with the issues of the people, but only to have his needs met. He is lavished with every good thing that his heart desires, as his people labor to keep him happy. A leader, on the other hand, has a purpose; a mission, to lead his people. He will guide them to the best of his knowledge and gives himself wholly to accomplish this task.

There were some kings in the Bible who had the title of king, but the heart of a leader. These kings pleased the Lord and He used them in mighty ways to further *"His Kingdom"* in the earth.

> *"Then all the tribes of Israel came to David at Hebron and spoke saying, 'Indeed we are your bone and your flesh. Also, in time past, when Saul was king over us, you were the one who led Israel out and brought them in; and the Lord said to you, 'You shall shepherd My people Israel and be ruler over Israel."(2 Samuel 5:1-2)*

The people referred to David as their leader, even though he was anointed king. God told David that he would shepherd His people. The word shepherd is defined as *one who herds, guards or tends sheep; one who cares for and guides a group of people, as a minister or a teacher*. This word is derived from the Hebrew word *raah***,** which means *to tend a flock, pasture it, to rule, to associate with, companion, keep company with, keep (sheep), keep(-er) or pastor*.

There has to be a separation of how the world views authority and how authority was intended to be used by God. To possess authority is a privilege, not a right. To be a leader, one should accept the responsibility with all of their heart and understand that they hold people's lives in their hands. As a leader, you should recognize the fragility of the people in whom you have authority over.

David was an actual sheepherder. He accepted this position of authority at a very young age and he worked at it with all of his heart. He was chosen by God to shepherd His people because of this.

Breaking the "Eve" Mentality

"So he shepherded them according to the integrity in his heart, and guided them by the skillfulness of his hands." (Psalm 78:72)

This is how God intends for those in authority to lead those under them. David understood how to lead the people of Israel through his experience of leading his sheep. I came across this text on the life of a sheepherder and this is how I see a real leader displaying his authority.

The duties of a shepherd in an unenclosed country like Palestine were very onerous. In the early morning, he led forth the flock from the fold, marching at its head to the spot where they were to be pastured. Here he watched them all day, taking care that none of the sheep strayed, and if any for a time eluded his watch and wandered away from the rest, seeking diligently till he found and brought it back. In those lands, sheep require to be supplied regularly with water, and the shepherd for this purpose has to guide them either to some running stream or to wells dug in the wilderness and furnished with troughs. At night he brought the flock home to the fold, counting them as they pass under the rod at the door to ensure himself that none were missing. Nor did his labors always end with sunset. Often he had to guard the fold through the dark hours from the attack of wild beasts, or the wily attempts of the prowling thief.

David, as a king and a leader, had many people under his authority and they respected him and submitted to him, because of his care for them and the guidance that he gave to them. He himself had to submit under authority to Saul, king before him. Saul became very fond of David and took him under his covering. Saul came to resent David, because of his character among the people. Saul knew that God was with David and this caused him to be afraid. Saul set out to kill David may times, but was unsuccessful, because the Lord was with David. Through all of this, David continued to submit to Saul, as his servant.

> *"Look, this day your eyes have seen that the Lord delivered you today into my hand in the cave, and someone urged me to kill you. But my eye spared you, and I said, 'I will not stretch out my hand against my lord, for he is the Lord's anointed."(1 Samuel 24:10)*

David displayed character that many of us in the world today do not know how to. No matter what Saul tried to do to him, he humbled himself and submitted to Saul's authority that was given to him by God. Even though Saul took advantage of that authority, David continued to submit, because he knew his place. David had been anointed king long before Saul tried to kill him, but he knew that there would be a process to go through before it was manifested. He did not swell up with pride and assume his position as king prematurely, the *"Eve Mentality"*. He waited on the Lord and it benefited David greatly.

The people of Israel submitted to David's authority when he became king, because of his willingness to submit to the authority over him. As a leader, whether it be on your job, in your home, in government, or in the church, you should first be able to submit yourselves before you expect others to submit to you. A pastor of mine once shared in a leadership meeting, *"What does the word leader mean to you?"* I sat there for a while and did not answer, because it was my first meeting and I was nervous, but the Holy Spirit said to me, *"Servant"*. The pastor went around the room and received different opinions on what a leader meant to them and it was over. That Sunday in church, he taught on leadership and shared with us the one word that a leader must be to his people and it was a *"Servant"*. I smiled and thanked the Holy Spirit for His leading, even though I was afraid to say it.

If you are reading this as a leader, I encourage you to humble yourself and ask yourself many questions. *Do I possess an attitude of a leader or a taskmaster? Do I care for the people I am over? Do I just worry about my own prosperity? Do I possess a servant's attitude? Do I seek for others to serve me?* Read over the life of David and watch how he matured over his lifespan to become *"the man after God's own heart"*.

If you are reading this and God is dealing with you on your reluctance to submit, I also urge you to look at the life of David. He understood that *ALL* authority comes from God and that no matter what it may look like in your life; submission is pertinent to your elevation. Humble yourselves, trust in the Lord your God, and break out of the *"Eve Mentality"*.

Prayer for Submission to Authority

Father we understand that it is difficult to submit to authority, because of pride in our hearts, but we know that with Christ we can do all things. I pray for us all to possess hearts like David's, Your servant. I thank You that each person reading this, whether it be leaders or those under them, will first of all submit to You, so that they will be able to submit to authority. Allow us to see that all that we do in this earth is in service to You. In Jesus' name. Amen.

Chapter 8
Submission in the Church

I'm saved…Now What?

I know that this topic of submission is not an easy one for many of us. I can attest to this myself, but I know that burdens are being removed even as you are reading this book, because they are also being removed from me as I write it. *GLORY TO GOD!* I pray that you will receive ALL that the Spirit is saying to you personally through these pages.

I believe that the most difficult place for people to submit is in the church. I say this, because the enemy understands how important a role submission plays in the body of Christ. We know from our pasts that it was like pulling teeth for us to get to a church, let alone give our lives to God. Even then, we were still *"straddling the fence"*; because we know that no one becomes new overnight. We see others in church Sunday after Sunday, and we see that they too have their faults. We understand that fellowship is necessary and we submit ourselves to them to account for our walk with God.

We have come to understand that, as Christians, we have been taught through many different teachings to submit to the different kinds of authority over us, because it pleases God. We feel as if we have reached a plateau in our personal walk with God, when out of nowhere, one of our leaders at church exercises their authority over us.

The car comes to a *screeching HALT!* The roller coaster suddenly *STOPS* in mid air! Your flesh begins to rise up and you say, *"You have got to be kidding me, who are you?"* We feel as if the person correcting us or giving us a bit of advice was the same one that went up to the altar last week. We say, *"Who is she (or he) to tell me that I need to do it over? They were a sinner just like me!"*

Have you said this before or at least thought it? I know that I have, because I have had my flesh rise up several times since I gave my life to the Lord. I am not ashamed to say it, because I realize that I am still flesh and not exempt from feeling this way. What we have to understand is that each of us has to go through a process and we may see other believers elevated before us. Please know that your goal when you become saved is to grow in the Lord and not to get a *position* in the church so you can say, *"I am Deacon so and so"*. This is not how God elevates us in the church. Your first priority should be to submit your life to Christ, so He can change you.

As time progresses, you will join different ministries within the church. You will begin to feel more comfortable and more apt to share your opinions. When you join a ministry, you receive the specifics of your duties *(Standard Order of Procedures)*. You go over them and agree that you will abide by these requirements and you join the ministry. Time passes and your leader asks you to see them after service. They proceed to tell you that you made a mistake or that you may need to sit down from the ministry for a time for whatever reason that they have given you.

THERE IT GOES; that look on your face that says, *"Excuse me? Who do you think you are?"* Your flesh rises up and now you are mad at the world. You begin to allow satan to fill your mind with all kinds of ungodly thoughts. Now, instead of receiving the constructive criticism or correction, you quit the ministry. This is a sure sign of immaturity in the body of Christ. You have to ask yourself, *"Why did I join this ministry?" "What was my motive in joining?"*

> *"Let nothing be done through selfish ambition or conceit, but in lowliness of mind let each other esteem others better than himself. Let each of you look out not only for his own interests, but also the interests of others."(Philippians 2:3-4)*

You have to see that when you are disobedient in your ministry, whether it be through irresponsibility or just not being willing to submit, you affect the whole ministry. When that leader allows you to join that ministry, they have to change things to make a place for you. Schedules are made, lesson plans are formed, practices are arranged, and now, because of your lack of commitment and your pride, you have caused confusion in the ministry. This is very dangerous people. We have to check ourselves often to see where we are in our walk with God.

> *"Examine yourselves as to whether you are in the faith. Test yourselves. Do you not know yourselves, that Jesus Christ is in you? _unless indeed you are disqualified?"(2 Corinthians 13:5)*

This is real my friend. Going to church is for you, not you for the church. The church was there before you came and it will have no problem being there when you leave! I beseech you to examine yourself *EVERYDAY*, so that you may be found blameless before the Lord. The enemy wants us to be divided in the body of Christ. Satan understands that when we truly come together in the house of God, he has no room for entry. He continues to plant seeds of discourse among the saints of God and we let him, because we *REFUSE* to submit, the *"Eve Mentality"*.

Put the enemy under your feet and instead of refusing to submit, *REFUSE* to be tricked by satan any longer. Trust the men and women of God that *He* has placed in authority over you. You complain about your leader's position, but God was the One that put them there. You have to be grounded in the Word of God.

> *"For exaltation comes neither from the east nor from the west nor from the south," (verse 7) "But God is the Judge: He puts down one, and exalts another."(Psalm 75:6-7)*

Therefore, if you want to complain to someone, which should not be your leader, you need to bring your issue before God, the *ELEVATOR*.

Put Your Hands to the "Plow"

Another thing that we fail to realize as babes in Christ, or even new members of a church is that the leaders before us had to go through a process as well. God does not elevate, unless He finds you faithful and even then, it is in His timing that He will prosper you. He knows what it will take and how long for each of us to be elevated.

> *"To everything there is a season, a time for every purpose under heaven."(Ecclesiastes 3:1)*

Meanwhile, you should be at work, doing God's business in the house. Where there is a need, fill it, no matter where it is. Many of us have heard some things from God concerning our purpose in this life and we run with it, instead of being still and waiting on Him to release us to it. When we are approached by a leader to serve in the house, let's say in the *"Unseen Hands"* ministry (cleaning the house of God) or the children's ministry, we say, *"Oh, I am sorry, but that is not where GOD has called ME to be." "HE revealed to ME my purpose, so I will wait on that."* Well my friend, I hate to be the one to tell you this *(no I am not)*, but you may be waiting a *LONG* time if you do not submit.

You have to be found faithful at work. The word work is defined as *the physical or mental effort or activity directed toward the production or accomplishment of something.* This word is derived from the Greek word *ergazomai,* which means *to toil, effect, be engaged in or with, commit, do, labor for, minister about, trade (by),work.* If God just handed us the vision for our lives, without us being prepared for it, we would fall on our faces. We have to be at work in the Kingdom, so that when He comes for us, we will be ready for it.

You will have already weathered many storms and will have come out on top. He will find that you have been faithful. The word faithful is defined as *adhering firmly and devotedly, as to a person, cause or idea; loyal; having or full of faith; worthy of trust or belief; reliable, consistent with truth or actuality.* This word is derived from the Greek word *pistos*, which means *trustworthy; trustful; believe (-ing, -r); faithful, sure, or true.*

If we are not faithful to our leaders, how can we be faithful to God? We talked previously about submission to authority in the *"world"*. We are natural beings and we should submit to our leaders in the world, so that we are able to submit to God.

> *"However, the spiritual is not first, but the natural, and afterward the spiritual."(2 Corinthians 15:46)*

So, do not believe that you can submit in the house of God, then go on your job and curse people out, because you would be lying to yourself. The only person that you are fooling is yourself, because the people on your job are calling you a hypocrite, because you have communicated (spoken) that you are a believer, but your actions are speaking otherwise. Now, because of your lack of submission, they see "the church" as a bunch of hypocrites and refuse to step a foot in the house of the Lord.

Again, submission runs a lot deeper than we realize. We think that we are just one believer and what *"I"* do will not affect the house, the *"Eve Mentality"*, but you are sadly mistaken. When we join a body, it is just that, a body. If you were to lose your leg, you would not be able to function properly. Every other body part is thrown off track in some way. When you join a ministry, you become connected in the Spirit to many other souls. When you become cut off, your brothers and sisters will be affected by it, because of the unity that is established in the heavenlies.

> *"from whom the whole body, joined and knit together by what every joint supplies, according to the effective working by which every part does its share, causes growth of the body for the edifying of itself in love." (Ephesians 4:16)*

There it goes again, *WORK!* It says by which *EVERY* part does its share. So, we see that wherever you are in the ministry, it is necessary for the growth of the church. Never discount your position in the church as *"unimportant"*, because we all serve as a piece to the puzzle.

Examine Yourself

I would like to share some things with you that I have experienced in my walk with God in this area. I was asked to join the dance ministry at my previous church and I was excited, because I had been praying for this opportunity in the ministry. My heart's desire was to minister in dance to the Lord. As time went on, I became stronger in this ministry, or at least I thought I was. My leader asked me to do a solo part to a dance and I was humbled, or at least I thought I was. I practiced this part for weeks and it was embedded in my spirit. All of a sudden, she switched parts and did the solo herself.

I could not believe that she had the audacity to remove me from this part! I had practiced this dance, until I could do it with my eyes closed. She began to teach me the other part of the dance and, in my flesh; I did not want to do it! Now mind you, I was smiling on the outside, but I was burning up on the inside. I do thank God for the foundation that I had received in Christ, because the Holy Spirit immediately quickened me to submit. I did not like it, but I did it, because I knew it was right and because I did, God was able to freely move in the midst of this ministry. I understood that if I would not have submitted, I could have caused division in this ministry. This was a test for me. My reaction would determine what God was able to trust me with, and therefore release into my hands.

> *"Now I urge you brethren, note those who cause divisions and offenses, contrary to the doctrine which you learned, and avoid them." (Romans 16:17)*

We have to make sure that we are in right relationship with the Father, so that this type of behavior will not manifest. In addition, we have to ask ourselves, *"Are we in ministry to give God the glory and do His business, or are we in ministry for the "status" that it may give to us?"* I can guarantee you that these "few" can cause confusion within the body of Christ. Their agenda and the agenda of the house are not the same.

> *"These are sensual persons, who cause divisions, not having the Spirit." (Jude 1:19)*

These people do not have a heart for ministry, but for the *"spotlight"*. Some are unwilling to submit to the leaders of the church, because they are jealous of the position. They serve their own visions, not the vision of the house. Therefore, God says to avoid these kinds of people, so that you will not be swept away with them.

Some Christians come to a church with an agenda. They may have held a position in their previous church and assume that they will have the same position in their new church. We have to be led by the Spirit people. There are many different seasons that we go through in our walk with God, and you may experience a season where God says, *"Sit Down"*, or serve in another position. I can attest to this, because I have been in that season. At first, I was very upset. I thought that I had done something wrong, but as I submitted and stepped down, God opened up a new opportunity for me in ministry. I could have just continued on doing what I was doing, but I would have been disobedient. I could have allowed confusion to come into that ministry. Instead, God used me as I had prayed to be used and the ministry flourished.

We have to understand that God is the One who elevates and He is the One who chooses who will be elevated. *DO NOT* seek to be elevated seek to *SERVE*. Our own Savior, Jesus Christ, even though He was King of kings and Lord of lords, served those around him. Therefore, your only agenda should be to serve in the church.

> *"When you are invited by anyone to a wedding feast, do not sit down in the best place, lest one more honorable than you be invited by him." (Verse 9) "and he who invited you and him come to you and say to you, "Give place to this man", and then you begin with shame to take the lowest place." (Verse 10) "But when you are invited, go and sit down in the lowest place, so that when he who invited you comes he may say to you, 'Friend, go higher.' Then you will have glory in the presence of those who sit at the table with you. (Verse 11) "For whoever exalts himself will be humbled, and he who humbles himself will be exalted."(Luke 14:8-11)*

We have to catch this revelation, so that we can avoid making errors and so that our church can prosper. No one in the church should have his or her own agenda, separate from the vision of the church. Yes, God gives us individual visions for our lives, but in the church there is one vision that is given to the shepherd of that house and you are there to *"support that vision, work for that vision, and SUBMIT to that vision!"*

> *"And if you have not been faithful in what is another man's, who will give you what is your own?" (Luke 16:2)*

So that vision that God has shown you, that one that you are trying to force into the house; you will not get it, unless you are faithful to your pastor's vision. Therefore, you need to check your motives, as a believer, to see if you are *"All About Him"* or *"All About You!"* as Eve was. This is real people. Our motives, as believers, should be *"All About Kingdom!!!"*

> *"But seek first the kingdom of God and His righteousness, and all these things shall be added to you." (Matthew 6:33)*

We should never seek for our own desires to be met if we have not submitted ourselves first to the Kingdom, which starts at your church. Now, we have covered why it is necessary to submit to the leaders in the church; ministry leaders, ministers, elders, deacons, etc. We will now discuss why it is important and crucial to submit to the *"head"* of the church, your pastor; your man or woman of God.

As I sought the Holy Spirit's guidance on this topic, He revealed to me that we *"say"* with our mouths that we can easily submit to our pastors, but if we cannot submit to the leaders under them, how are we *"truthfully"* submitting to our shepherd?

The Shepherd's Vision

We spoke of order back in Chapter 6 and we see now that there should be a clear order that is established in the house of God. Our pastors have a huge call on their lives to *"Feed the Flock"*. They rarely have time to spend with their own family, let alone deal with *EVERY* issue that comes about in the church. Yes, they are the Pastor, but this is why we have elders, deacons, ministers, etc., because they support our pastors in the vision that God has given them.

Our pastors will delegate authority to whomever God leads them to give it to and we, as believers, should respect it and receive it. We should be willing to receive the authority of our leaders, as if it were coming directly from the pastor's mouth.

> *"For this reason I left you in Crete, that you should set in order the things that are lacking, and appoint elders in every city as I commanded you."(Titus 1:5)*

This is Paul speaking to Titus advising him, or delegating to him, to set the church in order by appointing leaders who are faithful, who will serve in his absence, the people of God. Titus had to submit to Paul, who was submitting himself to the Will of God for his life, as well as the other believers. As Titus served Paul, the other believers whom he set as elders, submitted to him and taught the people.

This is order people and this is how God moves freely in a church. When everyone is in their proper *"position"*, signs, wonders, and miracles *WILL* take place. So, submit to your leaders as they submit to your Pastor. As I said before, God gives our pastors a vision in reference to their church. It is a specific vision that only that church can carry out. When you join a church, you go through a new member's orientation and receive an outline of the *VISION* of that house.

At this very moment, you have the choice to either reject it or submit to it. It is that simple! As believers, we are taught to be *LED* by the Spirit to join a church and know that this is where God has told you to plant yourself. Therefore, if you are *LED* to join, then the *VISION* should not be an issue, because God placed you there. *HALLELUJAH!* However, if you see that you cannot submit to the vision, then first you need to check yourself. Examine yourself to see what you have a problem with in the vision. I can guarantee you that the issue is *YOU*, not the vision!

Be Still and LISTEN!

The enemy always comes to confuse us when we have made a *RIGHT* decision. My husband and I moved from one Army community to another, for you military minded *(an ICOT)*. We were members of a wonderful church at our previous duty station and the move was only an hour away, so we chose to stay at the church. Well, two weeks later, on a Sunday morning, the Word of the Lord came and said, *"GO"! I am done with you here."* We were sad, but excited at the same time, because it was *HIM!* Therefore, we left the church and sought God on where to go next. I visited a church that was about ten minutes away from our new area, and I was definitely impressed, because the Word was there and the Spirit was evident. My husband was in the field *(military exercise)* and he urged me to visit and let him know what I thought. I did, but he was never *LED* to visit this particular church.

There was a church, also an hour away, in the opposite direction of our previous duty station. He was being led to visit this church, but every time, for about three weeks, we continued to miss a turn and somehow got lost. *"I"* became very frustrated and told my husband, *"Maybe God is not leading us here?"* He stood firm and told me that, *"This is our church."* We finally made it to the church and we joined that day. I had never seen my husband so in tune with the Word of God. His eyes were fixed on the *VISION* and he received it and submitted to it.

"I" could have led us in the wrong direction through my frustration, *"My issue"*, the *"Eve Mentality"*, but he, being the head, took the reigns and led us to our *"Promised Land"*. *GLORY TO GOD!* See men, you have *INFLUENCE! USE IT!*

Therefore, we see here that if we have an issue in ourselves, we can miss the vision that God is trying to place in our life. He uses the man of God, the one He gave the VISION to, to impart it; piece-by-piece, sermon-by-sermon, week-by-week, and even year-by-year into your life. We have to submit to our pastors, because they are the *"vessels"* in which the Spirit of God is released into our lives. An anointing is on the lives of our pastors and we can only receive it by staying *"Under"* them.

> *"And she had a sister called Mary, who also sat at Jesus' feet and heard His word." (Verse 40) "But Martha was distracted with much serving, and she approached Him and said, 'Lord, do you not care that my sister has left me to serve alone? Therefore, tell her to help me." (Verse 41) "And Jesus answered and said to her, "Martha, Martha, you are worried and troubled about many things." (Verse 42) "But one thing is needed, and Mary has chosen that good part, which will not be taken away from her."(Luke 10:39-42)*

This is so powerful! Do not get me wrong, serving is necessary, but we should be wise to know when we need to *"sit"* at our pastor's feet and receive a Word from the Lord. We can become so distracted, as Martha did, with all of the ministries that we have joined, that we lose sight of our spiritual growth. Many times, we commit to all of these different ministries, because we want to be *"recognized"* as the *"FAITHFUL"* member and desire for the pastor to notice us, therefore giving us an opportunity to get closer to them. I have to stop you here and warn you that this should *NOT* be your agenda. We should be seeking a closer relationship with God, not our pastors.

Mary understood that even though Jesus was in front of her, she was receiving directly from God, and because of this, the Word would not be taken away from her. Martha, on the other hand, was too busy trying to impress Jesus that she missed the real blessing.

Your Pastor, Not Your Friend

Our pastors are not impressed by the things that we do in the church, because they understand that your *SERVICE* is unto the Lord and not to them. They have caught this revelation, so now we need to so that we can stop making a fool out of ourselves. If you are serving for the right reasons, your reward will come from God, not from your Pastor.

> *"not with eye service, as men pleasers, but as bondservants of Christ, doing the will of God from the heart." (Verse 7) "with goodwill doing service, as to the Lord, and not to men."*
> *(Ephesians 6:6-7)*

I encourage you to receive this because if you do not, you will be setting yourself up for many disappointments in your walk with God. I know that we see others who walk side by side with the pastors and even the pastor's wives, but these are Spirit-led relationships, not just mere being his "boy" or her "girl". I mentioned before how our pastors are the *"vessels"* through which God sends revelation into our lives. When it is God's timing to elevate a believer, He will speak to their pastor. He may lead the pastor to take this believer under his wing to pour into their life. We have to stop seeking elevation and stay busy working in the Kingdom. We need to stop worrying about everyone else who is getting elevated and keep our eyes fixed on *JESUS!*

Luke 12:42-44 is an awesome example of staying busy. It says:

> *"And the Lord said, 'Who then is that faithful and wise steward, whom his master will make ruler over his household, to give them their portion of food in due season?" (Verse 43) "Blessed is that servant whom his master will find so doing when he comes." (Verse 44) "Truly, I say to you that he will make him ruler over all that he has."*

We all have a major role to play in the building of the Kingdom. Not even your Pastor's are greater than you in the eyes of God. God sees us all as His children. God does not give more of His love to our pastor, because he teaches us. He extends His love to us all.

> *"Then Peter opened his mouth, and said, 'Of a truth I perceive that God is no respecter of persons."(Acts 10:34, KJV)*

Now, do not take what I said and run with it. Your Pastor has a higher calling on his or her life than you may, and they are God's *"anointed"*. They are set apart to do something different from you. Do not take on the attitude with your pastor that says, *"You are a man just like I am"* or *"You are a woman just like I am"*. This is crossing the line and it is very dangerous. God will not accept this from you.

> *"Saying, Do not touch my anointed one's, and do my prophets no harm."(Psalm 105:15)*

God specifically tells us *"DO NOT"*, so this implies that there is a line that you do not cross. We understand that, yes, we are all flesh, but because of the *"calling"* on their lives, they have to guard themselves and be led by God to whom they should be joined together in fellowship with. The majority of pastors have only a few close friends in whom they can share intimate time with. Usually, another pastor or leader who has gained their trust is whom he or she finds to fellowship with him or her. Please be careful not to covet the life of a pastor, because many of us are *"ignorant"* to what this life truly requires.

Just Do It!

The man or woman of God over you is held accountable for every soul under his or her covering. They have to stay at the Father's feet to receive what *"Thus says the Lord"* for not only their family, but for what God is saying over your lives. Please respect their position and submit to them, so that God will reveal His purpose for your life through them. Oh, you thought that God would reveal your purpose to you when you cannot even submit to the vision of the church. It is *NOT* going to happen!

If you are unwilling to submit, and believe that you are hearing from God concerning His purpose for you, you are lying to yourself. Remember from Luke 16:12, we will not receive what is our *"own"* vision, unless we are faithful in another man's vision. Do not allow the enemy to deceive you. When we step out of line, the enemy comes in and can deceive us into believing that we are *"hearing"* from God or *"seeing"* visions that we are not. We should know that satan can also give us a *"vision"*.

> *"Again, the devil took Him up on high and showed Him all the kingdoms of the world and their glory."(Matthew 4:8)*

Satan took Jesus up high and showed Him what was below; the entire world He could have if He would worship him. Satan does this, so that we think God is elevating us, but God never brings you up to elevate you. He will lower you first, humble you, and prepare you for the elevation.

> *"Now this, 'He ascended"_what does it mean but that He also first descended into the lower parts of the earth?"*
> *(Ephesians 4:9)*

Jesus had to die first before He could be raised! *GLORY TO GOD!* Please hear what the Spirit is saying to us. Open your ears, your eyes, and your hearts to receive what God is trying to do in your life. He loves you; your pastors do as well, and they want you to receive *ALL* that God purposed for you to have.

Accept the authority of the leaders in your church and receive from them. I had to learn early on, some hard *"truths"* about myself as a believer concerning submission to my pastors. One instance that I am reminded of was when my first lady started an intercessory prayer group. It was designed to target specific prayer requests and things of that nature. One day she asked me to intercede specifically for something in the church and I agreed and did it. As I was interceding, I was led to a scripture that contradicted what she has asked me to pray for.

I was confused and called her to tell her what had happened and she corrected me and explained to me why this had happened.

As I explained earlier, I had pride in my heart that I was unaware of, but satan knew it. Instead of just submitting to my woman of God, and interceding for what she had asked of me, I allowed satan to *"show me a vision"*. Remember in Matthew 4 that satan took Jesus up and showed Him all that he would give Him if He would worship him. While I thought it was God leading me to this scripture, it was satan instead. He did not want me to intercede in this situation because he *KNEW* how I desired to submit to my first lady, but he had another plan and because of my *"ignorance"* in this area, I allowed him to do as he pleased. Through my naivety in the things of God, as well as the pride that was hidden inside of me, satan deceived me.

We have to know when God is speaking and when He is not! I told you that I was confused when I was taken to that scripture. Again, God *IS NOT* the author of confusion, but satan. The best way to know if it is God speaking is that you will have peace, not confusion. I ask you again to examine yourselves, test yourselves to see if there is something in you that needs to change. It is a sad fact to find out that the entire time you *"thought"* you were in the presence of God, you were not! Take it from me, it is a *HARD* pill to swallow, but I did and it allowed God to change me.

As I received her correction, which was the Lord's correction, because she is the Lord's anointed; I began to be broken in so many areas of my life. I felt as if the wrath of God came down from heaven on me! When you are being broken, it hurts! The *"ANOINTING"* is the only way that yokes can be destroyed, burdens removed, and souls set free. As I submitted to this brokenness, *"Did you hear that?"* I was finally submitting! Yokes were finally being destroyed in my life. This was absolutely the hardest thing that I have encountered in my life. Many people could turn away from God during a process like this, but I urge you not to do this, because the *"refining"* that takes place in you is worth it.

My father passed away when I was fourteen and I thought that it was the worst experience that I would have in my life, but this season in my life was the worst, as well as the best! The Lord was breaking me through her leading. I felt as if I were dying! I was, to myself. *GLORY TO GOD!* My flesh began to die as I submitted, not only to her, but also to the Will of God for my life. As you see, I *began* to die to self. This is definitely a *"process"* and it will last a lifetime.

> *"I affirm by the boasting in you which I have in Christ Jesus our Lord, I die daily."(1 Corinthians 15:31)*

I encountered this correction in several other instances with her and I saw, through submission and receiving from her, what God was doing in my life. Please saints of God, submit to your man or woman of God. Even if you do not see what they see right away, be obedient and do as they instruct you to do. God has revealed things to them, as His anointed, that you need to receive, but you will *"MISS IT"* if you are not willing to submit. Keep your eyes fixed on Jesus and the work of the Kingdom, the *"work"* that He has given *YOU* and humbly submit under the leadership of your Pastor.

> *"Obey those who rule over you, and be submissive, for they watch out for your souls, as those who must give account. Let them do so with joy and not with grief, for that would be unprofitable for you."(Hebrews 13:17)*

SELAH!

Prayer for Submission in the Church

Father, we thank You for *ALL* of the "nuggets" that You have revealed to us concerning submission in the church. We realize how cunning the enemy is and how he desires to divide us in the house of God, ultimately desiring for us to fall. We will not accept this, so we *WILLINGLY* choose to submit, not only to the leaders within our church, but also to the man and woman of God that You have placed over us. We will empower ourselves with the Word, so that we know when satan is on attack; therefore, being vigilant against his tricks. Our leaders are blessed! Our pastors are blessed! Our churches are blessed! We, the believers, are blessed! In Jesus' name. Amen.

Chapter 9
Submitting to the Will of God

"The Reason"

We have discussed many things in this book from the different types of submission to the spirits that hinder us from submitting. All of these topics were *NECESSARY* for us getting to this Chapter: *Submitting to the Will of God.*

No matter how hard we try, if we possess any of the aforementioned spirits or lack submission in any area of our lives, we cannot honestly submit to the Will of God. The definition for the word will is *a desire, purpose or determination, especially of one in authority; deliberate intention or wish; decree or ordain.* This word is derived from the Greek word *thelema*, which means *a determination, choice, decree, inclination, desire, pleasure, or will.*

We discussed why it is difficult for us to submit and we concluded that mainly, it is because of the *"I"* syndrome. This is our desire to want what we want and not have to answer to anyone, but ourselves, the *"Eve Mentality"*. We also concluded that it is impossible to get what God wants for us in this life, as well as the afterlife, without submission. We found that to receive the eternal, we must first submit to the natural; your spouse, your job, your government, and your leaders in the church.

Our Father is not just wise, *"He is Wisdom"!* He would not expect us to receive the spiritual things if we have not first received the natural things.

> *"And so it is written, 'The first man Adam became a living being, the last Adam became a life-giving spirit."*
> *(1Corinthians 16:45)*

Therefore, we need to be prepared in the natural to receive instructions on how to submit to the world before we can walk in submission to the Will of God.

I will use the example of marriage. How can a wife submit to the Father if she has refused to submit to her husband? As a woman, you cannot be *"sold-out"* to God and refusing to submit to your husband at the same time. This is a contradiction. How can you bypass your *"head"* to get to his *"Head"*? *GLORY TO GOD!* There is order to *EVERYTHING!* No one can bypass Jesus to get to the Father, so why do you think you can bypass your husband to get to Him.

> *"Jesus said to him, 'I am the way, the truth, and the life. No one comes to the Father except through Me."(John 14:6)*

I find it so amazing how we, as believers, progress towards submitting to the Will of God. Anything that is *"worth"* something requires work. We are not just all of a sudden going to submit once we become saved. It is a process. I believe that it takes such a long time *(sometimes a lifetime)*, because each time that we receive victory in an area, He receives the glory. We have to be broken many times throughout our lifetime, in order that we may continue to be humbled. We have to be taught how to become humble, it is not in us to do this automatically.

> *"Teach me to do your will, for You are my God, Your spirit is good. Lead me in the land of uprightness." (Psalm 143:10)*

We have to be led to do the Will of God and every area of submission that we have discussed previously, plays a part in this. We cannot submit in one area and refuse in another, because this is not the Will of God.

As we begin to put these acts of submission into play, we will see a huge change in our attitudes and our outlook on life. We will begin to see the blessings, or the *"fruit"*, of our willingness to submit. Our lives, our marriages, our jobs, and our walk with God will change before our very eyes and we will *"SEE"* that there is *NO* other way except to *SUBMIT!* Do not get me wrong, this is not an easy process. Submission is one of the hardest things to do, but as you make it your lifestyle, it will become like *"WORSHIP"* to you. You will desire to do *NOTHING* outside of the Will of God.

> *"I delight to do your will, O My God. And your law is within my heart." (Psalm 40:8)*

Once we catch this revelation, we will want to please Him in *ALL* things, which will lead us into His Will for our lives. You have to give something in order to get something! God gave His only Son to us, so that we could live in eternity with Him forever. *HALLELUJAH!*

What are You Waiting For?

I find that as we pray for God to reveal His Will for our lives, we do it doubtingly. We know that His Word says that if we ask then we will receive and if we knock, it will be opened, but we do not really believe this, if we are being honest with ourselves. The problem that we face as Christians is that we accept the *"MEDIOCRE"*. There are unbelievers who believe for more than we do! Why would an unsaved person want to give up *ALL* that they have in this world *(which is NOTHING)*, for just an *"ordinary"* life of a Christian? They do not *"see"* the examples of *"believers"* walking in dominion, as God would have us to.

> *"For all creation is waiting eagerly for that future day when God will reveal who His children really are." (Romans 8:19)*

We do not realize it, but that *"future"* day is *NOW!* God, in the Garden of Eden, gave Adam and Eve dominion on this earth. The earth is still here and we know that God's Word is established in heaven, so just because they messed up does not mean that His Word changes. God still desires for His Sons to walk in dominion in this earth, but if we just settle for mere *"crumbs"*, His Will cannot be revealed to us.

Back in Chapter 1, we saw how our decisions affect other people, not just ourselves. As believers, we are to be the manifested glory of God in this earth. Others should *"see"* us and ask, *"How do you and your spouse stay happy and in love?" "How can you be so calm when hell is all around us?" "How did you get what you have when it did not look like it could be done?"* The world is waiting; God is waiting, to see the Sons of God claim the dominion that He gave to them from the beginning!

When we recognize that we are His Sons, He will begin to reveal His Will to us. How can He reveal His Will if we do not even believe it? This would be pointless! We must first go through the process of building our faith, so we can *"see"* what God *"SEES"!*

> *"For My thoughts are not your thoughts, nor are your ways My ways, says the Lord."(Isaiah 55:8)*

So for us to receive *ALL* that He desires for us to have, we must first *BELIEVE*, then find out who He is. To know who He is, we must know His Word. His Will for our lives will not fall outside of His Word. Everything that we need in this life is found in the Spirit-filled pages of the Bible. If you think that you are walking in God's Will for your life and do not have a lifestyle of reading His Word, you are lying to yourself. So, if you desire to know the Will of God for your life, pick up your Bible and get to know your Father.

The word will, as we saw previously, has many different definitions. One was purpose, which is defined as *the object toward which one strives, or for which something exists; an aim or goal; intention or determination.* This word is derived from the Greek word *prothesis*, which means *a setting-forth; proposal (intention); the show-bread (in the Temple) as exposed before God: purpose; shew (-bread).* The purpose, the setting forth, the intention of God for us came through the body of Christ Jesus, our *"showbread"*.

In the days of the Levitical priesthood, no one could enter the most holy place, except the priests. They would prepare the tabernacle exactly how God instructed them to, so that He could dwell there. The table was prepared with the Bread of the Presence.

> *"You must always keep the special Bread of the Presence on the table before Me."(Exodus 26:30, NLT)*

This scripture reveals our purpose, *JESUS!* He is the *"show-bread"* that must be kept before the Father continually in order for God's Will to be revealed to us. *GLORY TO GOD!* Remember when I said, *"To know God, we must know His Word?"* The Word is *JESUS!* Every verse ever written in the Bible, Old and New Testament, refers somehow to Jesus. I would always read the Old Testament and ask myself, *"What does this have to do with being saved?"* Have any of you ever asked that question? Not until I received the Gift of the Holy Spirit did I begin to *"see"* Jesus in the Old Testament scriptures. Jesus has *ALWAYS* been there, we just have not seen it, because we have not had a real relationship with Him.

Many of us believed that He just popped up on the scene in Matthew 2, but He has forever been with us.

> *"In the beginning was the Word, and the Word was with God, and the Word was God. The same was in the beginning with God."(John 1:1-12, KJV)*

Jesus was and is the Word of God. From the beginning of scripture, Jesus is mentioned, as well as the Holy Spirit. We have been programmed to believe that Jesus was born and when He died, He left the *"Comforter"*, which is the Holy Spirit, with us and that was it. Genesis 1:3 says, *"And God said, 'Let there be light: and there was light."* The light is referring to Jesus: the *"LIGHT"* of the world".

Now, we have all heard of the Trinity: the Father, the Son and the Holy Spirit. For something to be triune, three in one, everything or everyone has to be together at the same time. *GLORY TO GOD!* The Father, the Son, and the Holy Spirit were all One in the beginning. In Genesis 1:1, 2 and 3, all parts of the Godhead are introduced.

Genesis 1:1 says, *"In the beginning God created the heaven and the earth."*

Genesis 1:2 says, *"And the earth was without form, and void; and darkness was on the face of the deep. And the Spirit of God was hovering over the face of the waters."*

Genesis 1:3 says, *"Then God said, "Let there be light, and there was light."*

My God, the first three verses of the Bible show clearly that they, being One, were together in the beginning. We have been saved for years and have never *"seen"* this Truth. This is why the Holy Spirit is *NECESSARY*, so that we can have this revelation. Genesis 1:1 says that *GOD* created the heavens and the earth. Genesis 1:2 shows the Spirit hovering over the waters, *the Holy Spirit*, and Genesis 1:3 is where the Light of the world is introduced, which represents *JESUS!!!! GLORY TO GOD!* There is more revelation in those first three verses than we can ever know!

Another definition of will was to determine, which is defined as *to decide or settle, conclusively or authoritatively*. This word is derived from the Greek word *horizon*, which means *to mark out or bound (horizon); to appoint, decree, specify: declare, determine, limit, or ordain*. God has determined some things for our lives from the beginning of the world.

> *"Before I formed you in the womb I knew you; before you were born I sanctified you; I ordained you a prophet to the nations."(Jeremiah 1:5)*

God said He ordained Jeremiah to be a prophet, He *determined* beforehand what the order of Jeremiah's life would be. God has a predestined plan for your life; one that He *"marked out"* before you were born that you would walk in it. So, if you are trying to find your purpose in this life, outside of the Will of God, you will live a frustrating life, because He already appointed a life for you. *GLORY TO GOD!*

Many of us go through life with no joy? We are not satisfied with what we have, causing us to change everything about our lives from our jobs, to our spouses. We cannot stay in one job for too long, because we become bored or we become unsatisfied with our salary. We switch from partner to partner in marriage, because they do not make us happy anymore or we feel like they are not giving us what we want, the *"Eve Mentality"*. We have to realize that if we have no joy in ourselves, nothing or no one can give it to us, but God. We will continue on this path if we do not accept God's Will for our lives.

"And truly the Son of Man goes as it has been determined, but woe to that man by whom He is betrayed."(Luke 22:22)

God determined the walk of Jesus on this earth and He has also determined your walk. So, let us find out how to walk in it!

God has SPOKEN!

We know the reason that Jesus was sent to the earth, to be a sacrifice for our sins, so that we may give our lives over to Him and live eternally with Him. So, when we do give our lives over, become saved, we also have a purpose that God has willed.

"Go therefore and make disciples of all the nations, baptizing them in the name of the Father, the Son and of the Holy Spirit."(Matthew 28:19)

This is the Great Commission given to us by Jesus before He died on the cross. The word commission is defined as *the act of granting certain powers or the authority to carry out a particular task for duty*. This word is derived from the Greek word *epitrope*, which means *permission, full power; commission*.

Jesus asks us in this scripture to *"carry out"* a particular task or duty that He needs for us to accomplish; to make disciples of *ALL* nations. This is our *"job"* on this earth; God's Will for the believer; to spread the Word, so others will believe also. This is His decree to us. The job that you have in the natural is just a means of supplying you with the finances needed to fulfill His purpose in this earth. *HALLELUJAH!*

Another meaning of the word will was desire, which means *to wish or long for; want*. This word is derived from the Greek word *epizeteo*, which means *to search (inquire) for, to demand, to crave, desire, inquire, seek (after, for)*. There are many things that we seek after, or desire, in this world; including jobs, money, spouses, cars, homes, etc. We make the mistake of praying and asking for these things in accordance to God's Will when God has already supplied all of our need according to His riches in glory in Christ Jesus.(Philippians 4:19)

> *"But seek first the kingdom of God and His righteousness, and all these things shall be added to you." (Matthew 6:33)*

The scripture says *SEEK*, or *DESIRE*, the Kingdom *FIRST!* Our problem is that we are seeking the *"things"* first. We want God to bless us, but we are not willing to submit to Him and work in the Kingdom. The scripture says seek first the Kingdom of God and His righteousness and the *"things"* will come. We cannot change the Word of God to suit our needs. It *WILL NOT* work!

You may begin to see the *"things"* come, but if you are not seeking Him, they *ARE NOT* from Him!

> *"You will show me the path of life; in Your presence is fullness of joy; at Your right hand are pleasures forevermore." (Psalm 169:11)*

Therefore, we see that in His presence we have pleasures forevermore, not temporarily. If we are seeking His Will for our lives, not our own, He will begin to open many doors for us. If we commit daily to meditate on His Word, have a consistent prayer life, commit to the work of the Kingdom, and give freely and willingly into it, God cannot help but bless us. I know that we have many desires, but God desires greater for us than we could ever imagine for ourselves. He has a greater expectation of us than we have of ourselves.

> *"Now to Him who is able to do exceedingly abundantly above all that we ask or think, according to the power that works in us." (Ephesians 3:20)*

We do not even have to ask for it. If we think that we want something, God says He can do exceedingly and abundantly greater than you can think. That is *AWESOME!* The thoughts that I have for my family and myself are *NOTHING* compared to what His thoughts are for us. This is why we need to seek His Will, so that we will have joy in our lives and not frustration. When we have purpose in life, we wake up every morning expecting God to do something miraculous in our lives. As we believe that He is doing this daily, our faith begins to increase.

Many times, as Christians, we feel as if we are not walking in His Will. Just because we do not *"see"* the manifestation of some things, does not mean that we do not have it, because we do. What we lack is patience to endure until God says, *"It is time"* to receive what He has *already* stored up for you. There will be times in your life that will feel like *"wilderness"* experiences. In these times, God is trying to purge some things from us in order for us to receive and *'hold on to"* the blessing. Stand firm, remain focused, and *KNOW* who He is and what His Word says and submit to His Will.

Dominion: Our Earthly Inheritance

The last thing that we will discuss concerning the Will of God is why we were placed here in the beginning. We discussed several times throughout this book the issue of dominion. Again, we will go back to Genesis 1:28, which says,

> *"Be fruitful and multiply; fill the earth and subdue it; have dominion over the fish of the sea, over the birds of the air, and over every living thing that moves on the earth."*

The word dominion as we said before means *to subjugate; to tread down; to prevail against; to reign or rule*. God wants us, as He wanted Adam and Eve, to have *"dominion"* in this earth. He purposed from the beginning for us to walk in all power, authority, and prosperity, but we have allowed the *"world"* to have what is rightfully ours. Eve gave her dominion over to the serpent, which caused the *"power-shift"*, if you will.

God's will has not changed. My pastor taught us not too long ago on this subject and explained to us that God is trying to get us back to the beginning, the Garden of Eden. He wants us to see ourselves as He *"saw"* us in the beginning. As believers, we need to walk in dominion and claim our inheritance here on this earth. We are striving to get to heaven before we fulfill His Will here on earth.

We do not understand the scriptures correctly. We have an *"inheritance"* right here on earth if we would just receive it.

> *"As for every man to whom God has given riches and wealth, and given him power to eat of it, to receive his heritage and rejoice in his labor--this is the gift of God." (Ecclesiastes 5:19)*

God's Will for us in this earth is to receive the wealth that is stored up for us and use it in the furthering of His Kingdom here on the earth. We received the Great Commission to go into all nations and spread the Gospel of Jesus Christ. How can we do this without *"wealth"*? God desires for His children to rise up in this world and show His glory through their lives. Many of us Christians are not doing this. We are walking around broke and trying to witness to unbelievers who are better off financially than we are! Why would they want to be a *"believer"*? What are we showing them to believe in, being broke? We are ineffective witness's people if we are not out of debt and walking in the *"OVERFLOW"* that God intended for us to have.

Non-believers should look at us and *"SEE"* something different. They should desire to have what we have as children of the Most High God!

> *"Let your light so shine before men, that they may see your good works and glorify your Father in heaven."*
> *(Matthew 5:16)*

We, as believers, should be the manifested glory of God in the earth. If we are children of the Almighty God, then we need *"look"* the part. How else will you be distinguished from a non-believer? What we need to recognize is that you say you are a believer, but can God tell that you are His? If God cannot even recognize you as His sons, how can the world?

Stop allowing the enemy to hold you back from receiving your inheritance as a child of God. The real enemy is not satan; it is your *"unbelief"*. We give the devil more power than he actually has. Satan has less power than our *"weakest"* qualities as a child of God. We give him power, just as Eve gave him dominion over her inheritance. Every time that we choose to go in debt, we give our *"inheritance"*, or wealth, over to the enemy, the *"Eve Mentality"*.

> *"In Him also we have obtained an inheritance being predestined according to the purpose of Him who works all things according to the counsel of His Will."(Ephesians 1:11)*

God has a purpose for us here on earth and that is to bring people into the knowledge of His Son. For us to do this effectively, we need to be financially stable. When we frivolously use the money that God has given to us, we *"insult"* Him. Our jobs that we were blessed with by God are not for us! The financial gain that we receive from that job is also not for us! The Holy Spirit revealed to me that the money that we receive from our jobs is to first, give our tithes and offerings back to God. Secondly, our earnings should be used for helping the needy, the poor, and bringing the Gospel to the nations. Our finances are not for us! You ask, *"So how am I supposed to pay my bills?* Have faith? Remember, God said seek first the Kingdom of God and all these things shall be added unto you.

> *"And my God shall supply all your need according to His riches in glory by Christ Jesus."(Philippians 4:19)*

God is our *"SUPPLIER"!* He is the *ONE* who gives us the power to get wealth (Deuteronomy 8:18). If you have *"faith"*, then you will trust God to supply you with the necessary funding to pay your bills and get the *"things"* that you desire. You have to be faithful with what He has already given to you before He will bless you with more. Never seek yourself first, but others. This is the heart of God! When we catch a hold of this revelation, we will walk in *DOMINION*. As we remain faithful, God will continue to elevate us to higher levels; therefore, causing those under us to be elevated as well.

There *WILL* be a people in this earth who will *"show forth"* God's glory. There *WILL* be a people in this earth who have God's *FAVOR*. There *WILL* be a people in this earth who will walk in *DOMINION!* Will *"you"* be one of them?

Empower yourselves with the Word, receive deliverance from debt; use it for the furthering of His Kingdom (spreading the Gospel) and walk in the *DOMINION* that He created you to walk in. Be the praise of His glory! The Will of God is simple if we allow to it to be. Do the Will of God in this earth; everything else that you get along the way are just blessings, *"the things"*, from being submissive to His Will by seeking the *"KINGDOM FIRST"!*

<u>*Prayer for Submitting to the Will of God*</u>

Father, we thank You for who You are. We thank You for sending Your Son Jesus Christ to die for our sins so that we might live eternally with You. You are the Alpha and the Omega, our beginning and our end. We receive Your Will for us right now and purpose to walk in the dominion that You gave to us, Your people.

We will be the light in the midst of this dark world and will be Your manifested glory in the earth. We will seek your Kingdom first and do the "work", until the day you call us home. We thank You in advance for supplying *ALL* of our need according to Your riches in glory by Christ Jesus. In Jesus' name. Amen.

Chapter 10
Victory Through Submission

Know That You "Know"

We have tackled a great deal concerning submission in this book. We have dissected the root causes of why we were unable to submit and now have *True Knowledge* in dealing with this issue head on. We have empowered ourselves through the Word of God and through understanding the *"REAL"* meanings of the words used in this text, as God sees them. We should now be able to walk in *VICTORY*, because we have obtained the knowledge necessary to do so. The word victory is defined as *the defeat of an enemy or opponent; success in a struggle against difficulties or an obstacle; the state of having triumphed.* This word is derived from the Greek word *nikao*, which means *to subdue, conquer, overcome, prevail, or get the victory.*

We have received *VICTORY* through *submission!* We have defeated it, triumphed over it, subdued it, conquered it, prevailed against it, and overcome it! We have the *VICTORY*, because we believe His Word.

> *"For whatever is born of God overcomes the world. And this is the victory that has overcome the world--our faith."(1 John 5:4)*

We have taken how the *"world"* defines submission and put it under our feet. We now know how God views submission and how we are to submit in *EVERY* realm of life, which gives us power and authority over the enemy.

We know that both power and authority are derived from the Greek word *exousia*. We have *EXOUSIA* in the earth believers and we need to act on it and walk in it! A dear sister-in-Christ of mine was given a vision by God to start a website where believers could go and find products and services that will empower them with the resources needed to help them live abundantly the life that God intended for them, and to advance the Kingdom of God to glorify Him. The website is theexousia. This site allows us the peace in knowing that if we type in a topic for research, that we will not pull up anything derogatory, as the search engines do. She has set her vision apart from the world's vision by submitting to the Will of God for His people. She has the *VICTORY!* It is already done, because she took the road of submission.

What vision has God given to you that you need to submit to? Receive your *VICTORY* as well. The vision that God gave to His Son Jesus Christ was fulfilled, because of His submission to the Father.

> *"He went a little farther and fell on His face, and prayed, saying, 'O, my Father, if it is possible, let this cup pass from Me; nevertheless, not as I will, but as You will."(Matthew 26:39)*

The Word says He *"went a little farther"*, which means He *"pressed"* forward and then prayed. We have to do something first before God will step in. We received the *VICTORY*, because of this statement. Jesus carried out the vision no matter what the cost was. Winston Churchill said it this way:

> *"Victory at all costs, victory in spite of all terror, victory however long and hard the road may be."*

This should be our confession as believers in Christ because, in essence, this was His confession as He lay before God in the Garden of Gethsemane; *"Not as I will, but as You will"*. We have to know who has gone before us and what He has already done for us. He laid His life down, so that we may have the *VICTORY*! He defeated satan at the cross.

> *"O sing to the Lord a new song! For He has done marvelous things: His right hand and His holy arm have gained Him the victory."(Psalm 98:1)*

We know that we are joint heirs with Christ, so because He received the *VICTORY*, we too have received it! Christ was the *"EXAMPLE"* of submission for us. He was made low for our benefit. This was true humility. We have to remain humble through every test and trial to keep the *VICTORY*! Never believe that you have reached a level of submission where you can submit no more, because every test in life requires submission.

Now that you have the knowledge of what submission means and the many different ways to submit, satan will try you. He will send many different obstacles your way to see if you really believe that you have the *VICTORY*! Satan is a twister of the *TRUTH*, so we have to be empowered by the Word to counteract his lies. Know the Word of God; know Jesus!

"So shall my Word be that goes forth from My mouth; It shall not return to me void. But it shall accomplish what I please, and it shall prosper in the thing for which I sent it."(Isaiah 55:11)

God is telling us to give His Word back to Him; the Word is Jesus! When we submit to the Word, we begin to become *"like"* the Word. We need to imitate Jesus. We need to walk like Him, talk like Him, look like Him, smell like Him, see like Him, touch like Him_live like HIM! *GLORY TO GOD!* Just as Jesus prospered in the thing for which He was sent to do, we will prosper and have *VICTORY* in the purpose that we were put here for by becoming more like Him everyday. It is in Him that we have received eternal life. It is in Him that we have been made righteous. It is in Him that we have received the *VICTORY!*

"But thanks be to God who gives us the victory through our Lord Jesus Christ."(1 Corinthians 15:57)

We cannot receive victory through any other channel, except Jesus! The Word says it!

We Shall OVERCOME!

We saw that the Greek derivation of victory was *nikao*. One of the definitions given for *nikao* was *to overcome*. Overcome is defined as *to defeat (another) in competition or conflict; conquer, to prevail over; to surmount opposition or victorious*. We should not fear for anything or anyone in this life. We have the *VICTORY*, because Jesus *OVERCAME* the world.

"These things have I spoken to you, that in Me you may have peace. In the world you will have tribulation, but be of good cheer; I have overcome the world."(John 16:33)

Breaking the "Eve" Mentality

The world will scoff at us for being submissive and call us many names, but stand firm and press on! They expect us to do as they do, but we are no longer like them. We have changed partners and our eyes have been opened to the schemes of the enemy. Never fear what the *"world"* may say to you about your faith. They see something in you that they want for themselves.

> *"You are of God, little children, and have overcome them, because He who is in you is greater than he who is in the world."(1 John 4:4)*

Continue to be consistent in your walk with God, so that *"those who are in the world"* will see your good works and glorify God.

There are several instances in Revelation where the seven churches are being spoken to concerning the areas that they refused to submit in or the areas that they needed to continue in. They were given assurance that if they heard what the Spirit was saying to them, and overcame, that they would receive their *VICTORY!*

The Church of Ephesus, Revelation 2:7 says, *"He who has an ear, let him hear what the Spirit says to the churches. To him who overcomes, I will give to eat from the tree of life, which is in the midst of the Paradise of God."*

The Church in Smyrna, Revelation 2:11 says, *"He who has an ear, let him hear what the Spirit says to the churches. He who overcomes shall not be hurt by the second death.*

The Church in Pergamos, Revelation 2:17 says, *"He who has an ear, let him hear what the Spirit says to the churches. To him who overcomes I will give some of the hidden manna to eat. And I will give him a white stone, and on the stone a new name written which no one knows except him who receives it."*

The Church in Thyatira, Revelation 2:26-29 says, *"And he who overcomes, and keeps My works until the end, to him I will give power over the nations." (Verse 27), "He shall rule them with a rod of iron; They shall be dashed to pieces like the potter's vessels'_as I also have received from My Father." (Verse 28), "and I will give him the morning star." (Verse 29), "He who has an ear to hear, let him hear what the Spirit says to the churches."*

The Church in Sardis, Revelation 3:5-6 says, *"He who overcomes shall be clothed in white garments, and I will not blot out his name from the Book of Life; but I will confess his name before My Father and before His angels." (Verse 6), "He who has an ear, let him hear what the Spirit says to the churches."*

The Church in Philadelphia, Revelation 3:12-13 says, *"He who overcomes I will make him a pillar in the temple of My God, and he shall go out no more. I will write on him the name of My God and the name of the city of My God, the New Jerusalem, which comes down out of heaven from My God. And I will write on him My new name."* (Verse 13), *"He who has an ear, let him hear what the Spirit says to the churches."*

The Church of the Laodiceans, Revelation 3:21-22 says, *"To him who overcomes I will grant to sit with Me on My throne, as I also overcame and sat down with My Father on His throne." (Verse 22), "He who has an ear, let him hear what the Spirit says to the churches."*

All of these churches from the faithful to the dead were given a promise from God that if they overcame their obstacles, or continued to be faithful, He would give them *VICTORY!* We have to understand that overcoming submission and gaining *VICTORY* in it will lead us to the Promises of God! *HALLELUJAH!*

Again, the word victory is defined as *the defeat of an enemy or opponent or success in a struggle against difficulties or an obstacle.* We will continue in this life to have enemies and the struggles will continue to come up, but we have to defeat them and gain success in them one-by-one. Know that Jesus has already gained the *VICTORY* over satan; *BELIEVE IT* and *WALK IN IT!*

Notice that I have not used the phrase the *"Eve Mentality"* in this chapter so far. The reason is that I *BELIEVE*, through the knowledge and revelation of God's Word and the guidance of the Holy Spirit that we have *BROKEN* the spirit of the *"Eve Mentality"* and received *VICTORY THROUGH SUBMISSION! IT IS DONE!*

Prayer For Victory through the act of Submission

Dear Heavenly Father, we thank You for the *VICTORY!* We *REFUSE* to allow the enemy to rule over our lives any longer. We thank You for breaking the *"Eve Mentality"* over our lives. We willingly submit ourselves under Your Mighty hand, which allows us peace in every area of our lives. We know that submission is the key to us living the lives of peace that you intended for us to walk in when you Created us. Thank You for Your redemptive work through Your Son Jesus Christ, which now gives us a Way to You.

We understand the *NEED* for submission in this world; because it brings order into such chaos that we now live in. We thank You that our *Marriages are BLESSED, our Jobs are BLESSED, our Government is BLESSED, our Relationships are BLESSED, our Churches are BLESSED and yes, we are BLESSED,* because we have willingly submitted in each area of our lives. Bring us back to the beginning and show us, Your people, that we have *DOMINION* in this earth. We *WILL* be Your manifested glory in this earth. We have the *VICTORY THROUGH OUR LORD AND SAVIOR JESUS CHRIST!* In Jesus' name. Amen.

Notes

Chapter 3

Page 25: Quote from Benjamin Franklin taken from Oxford World's Classic: Benjamin Franklin Autobiography and other writings: Edited with an Introduction and notes by Ormond Seavey.

Chapter 7

Page 93: Life of a Shepherd taken from Easton's 1897 Bible Dictionary.

Chapter 10

Page 131: Quote from Winston Churchill taken from "Winston Churchill", by Henry Pellin.

*Other titles by Inspirational Author
Deborah G. Hunter*

THE CALL OF INTERCESSION

Book Sold on Amazon.com and BarnesandNoble.com

ISBN 13: 978-0-9823944-3-4
$14.99

Debbie Hunter is an extraordinary Christian woman who has made her life's assignment the pursuit of intercessory dimensions. As readers engage The Call of Intercession, they are taken on a journey into the private and holy chambers of the heart of this author who, by the aid of the Holy Spirit, is able to express the mind of God as it relates to this unique and significant assignment of prayer and intimacy with God.

~Dr. Keira Taylor-Banks
Executive Pastor, Living Waters Christian Fellowship
Newport News, Virginia

The Call of Intercession is a clarion call to the Body of Christ to intercede for the nations of this world, as well as for what is on the heart of God in this hour. Intercessors are being sent by God to cry out on behalf of the earth, and they need to know how to operate in their gifting, as well as know the order in the Body of Christ. Will you answer the call?

~Deborah G. Hunter

If you are an aspiring Christian writer, or an already published author looking to further market your message to the world, visit our website and contact us for an initial phone consultation.

Publisher_Hunter Heart Publishing
www.hunterheartpublishing.com

www.ingramcontent.com/pod-product-compliance
Lightning Source LLC
Chambersburg PA
CBHW070156100426
42743CB00013B/2934